The photo you see above is the image from the cover of the September 1920 *Inspiration* newsletter that was published by the Woman's Institute of Domestic Arts and Sciences which inspired my book *Vintage Notions*. For a more modern look I chose to update this edition with the cover artwork from the August, 1923 issue of the Woman's Institute *Fashion Service* magazine.

SEPTEMBER *Inspiration* 1920

Edited by GUSTAVE L. WEINSS

Preparations for Service

BY THE EDITOR

NOW comes the time of the year when activities in nearly all lines of endeavor are resumed with new vigor. The school bells have sounded, calling teachers and scholars back to their studies; vacations are practically over, permitting the problems of home life and business to be taken up again with unbroken sequence; the very air seems to have become charged with an impelling influence, inspiring one and all to renew efforts that were more or less hampered in the summer months.

It is undoubtedly good for all of us to pass through a period that calls for a certain amount of relaxation. Changes of this kind are conducive to mental balance. They permit us to look into our future and to plan and prepare for the service that we must give if we would achieve success.

SERVICE. What a magnetic word this is nowadays! At one time one who served was looked upon as a slave, as a menial. To offer service placed one in a lower stratum of society. Now business firms are vying with one another to see which can render the best service to their customers; schools and colleges are exerting extraordinary efforts to provide for their students that service which will enable them to cope with life in all its phases; individuals are coming to the realization that "he fares best who serves best." Everywhere we look we see the banner of service leading the procession of the earnest and the prosperous.

IF YOU read between the lines of present-day announcements of progressive institutions, you will quickly perceive that they are engaged in undertakings that bespeak much for the future good of themselves and those they wish to serve.

They realize that the war years of arrested development have set them back and that they must speed up to meet present demands, as well as anticipate the needs of years ahead. But right preparation will enable them not only to give immediate service, but to increase their service as time goes on.

And what better thought can we as individuals have for ourselves? In preparing our minds and our hands to render service for the good of others, we put ourselves in a condition to serve immediately and to improve our service as we strive.

IT IS along these lines that the Institute has been advancing since its inception. Ever since we began to teach we have had the thought of service to our students uppermost in mind. Was there a change to be made, it was considered from the angle of whether or not it would mean better service for our students. Was a new policy to be inaugurated, it was put forth with the idea of rendering better service. Preparation for service has been, is, and will continue to be our policy. We learn from experience, and as we learn we aim to give our friends the benefit of the knowledge we acquire.

DURING the past few weeks we have been preparing for distribution to our dressmaking students a book that will be of extreme value to them. This book we call the "Woman's Institute Fashion Service." It contains authentic styles in dresses, suits, coats, and wraps for the fall and winter season of 1920-1921. There is also text matter explaining each one of the illustrations and its variations, which should enable Institute students to make for themselves clothes that will carry with them the consummation of ideas of expert designers here and abroad.

Our hope, with this Fashion Service, which will be published in the spring and fall of each year, is simply to enhance the value of the service we already extend and thus enable our students to be of greater service to themselves and others.

SO, in harmony with the spirit of progressive firms and individuals, it is of paramount importance for all those who are the least inclined to indecision to prepare for the service they must render if they would reap the reward of industry.

It requires courage and ambition to plan and prepare for the rendering of real service. Some are too much inclined to remain at a standstill, thinking that what they now do is sufficient and trying to make themselves believe that it is all right to let good enough alone. But that is where they err.

The call of today is for progress. No one, great or small, unless he is content to trail behind, dare ignore this call. The ambitious will keep on progressing, knowing that the preparations they make for service today will aid them on the morrow.

Happy Thinking

By MARY BROOKS PICKEN
Director of Instruction

HAPPINESS is such a big, generous, understandable word that I really delight in using it. I sat the other day, feeling much depressed, and unconsciously my pencil wrote *H-a-p,* and then it seemed the other letters needed to spell *happiness* just naturally connected themselves to these first three letters. When I glanced at the paper and saw the word complete, I was interested. I was not conscious of having written it. Just seeing the word made me smile and the smile brought cheerful reflections, and soon I was surrounded by happy thoughts.

THE word and its effect reminded me of a similar circumstance that a friend told me about. This friend had gone to bed thoroughly discouraged and burdened with self-pity. As she was lying there, magnifying every conceivable discomfiture, she heard a member of the household arguing with a man who had a big cartload of sand to deliver, the man insisting that the sand belonged at this friend's number. She looked out of the window and saw the sand, and her sense of humor immediately became evident. Sand! That was exactly what she needed, a mental sand tonic to stimulate her appreciation and to increase her tolerance.

The sand was delivered at a corresponding number in the next block, but the driver, unknowingly, had accomplished a good deed, for the humor of the situation brought smiles, and smiles always eradicate worry wrinkles.

RECENTLY I went to see a very good friend who had lost her daughter and whose son had moved across the continent. Knowing this mother's great affection for her two children, I dreaded conversation with her, feeling that she would be grieved and not happy. I said when starting that I would do almost anything rather than go. But I went and I stayed three whole hours. We talked about fruit, flowers, the school problems, and we discussed our cherished authors. Then we talked of astrology and astronomy, God and nature. I never had a more delightful visit.

I never went home feeling happier and more enthusiastic. But when I arrived there, the folks began to sympathize with me, thinking that I had spent an unpleasant evening, and then I remembered how I felt when I started out. Was it possible that this delightful woman had so recently known a great grief! As I thought about it, I marveled at her power of adjustment, her poise, her command of herself. She, a cultured woman, capable of the finest feelings, had endured so much! But she was my hostess, and she felt it her duty to make me happy, and in doing it she was benefited, for she verily radiated happiness and good cheer.

A LETTER of several pages came to my desk the other day, and as it was such a happy letter I read it three times. Like cool water, it actually refreshed me. For instance, this paragraph:

"Whenever I hear people talking about homekeeping being so 'drab,' I wonder why all women, even those with large families, do not find some little side issue that to them spells 'play,' and then play a little all along the way. I've always been blessed with a keen imagination, so that I could see gardens and castles even if I lived in a desert, couldn't you?"

And then this:

"I must not close until I tell you something of the delightful time I am having this season. At first I worked on the sewing samplers after I had done a day's work (and sometimes more) of sewing for other people. Now I start out the other way. Each morning I'm taking two hours for study before I open up my sewing. I knew all the time that I should do this, but I felt rushed for time. I soon found that I'd gain time by knowing more, so the busier I get from now on the more I shall study and apply my Dressmaking lessons.

"I was amazed to learn that people are always eager for thinking dressmakers—those who can help them plan their garments. One lady brought materials for four fall dresses for herself and three daughters, saying, 'You design them and make them as they should be for us.' So I had the pleasure of planning every detail of each one. When I explained my plan for the embroidery and other decorations, she said, 'Yes, I like your ideas. It's a delight to find some one who can help me plan clothes so satisfactorily.' And, Mrs. Picken, last month I added sixty whole dollars to my 'Kitchen Fund.'"

ONLY the other day I read of a housewife who has found it necessary to do all her own housework for the first time in her experience. She writes thus:

"I decided to master my work, not to allow my work to master me. I determined to treat work respectfully and to insist upon respectful treatment from my work. Instead of employing the breathing intervals in my day's routine in complaining of the hardships of my lot, I lived every spare moment in the inspiring company of good books. If I stopped a moment to rest my arms from sweeping, I had a word with Browning. While I stirred my cake, Keats was within communing distance. I found time to look away for a moment from the most homely task. Matthew Arnold, Tennyson, and a distinguished group of poets and essayists were always ready to respond to my call for inspiration and help me to live above the routine of the day's work.

"I am called a good housekeeper, an excellent cook. I consider it high credit; and I trust and believe that it is credit to which I am entitled. I cannot say that I have learned to regard housework with consuming affection; but I dare say that I have come to get great and peculiar satisfaction from the consciousness that I can do housework year in and year out, do it well, and at the same time keep in vital and intimate contact with the finest expressions of human inspiration and wisdom. I know the joy that comes at night from honest and efficient discharge of the day's work. The degree of the work has ceased to trouble me. All useful and necessary work fits into the great scheme of things. Emerson did his work; I do mine. We are comrades. The spirit of usefulness joins us in the great freemasonry of service."

THIS woman evidences that she is not by any means one of the kind who literally pinch themselves to feel the hurt. It is surprising how many, many of this latter type one finds even among one's friends,—people who will hug imaginary or magnified hurts, who will insist upon reminiscing over sadnesses, anticipating misfortunes, instead of filling each hour with pleasant thoughts, wholesome, healthy thoughts that will keep them alert and mentally ready for emergencies. A happy thinking mind is a veritable antidote for mistakes and worries. Happy thinking people are always good company for themselves, as well as delightful companions for other folks.

BRUCE BARTON has written an editorial that I have read often. The title is, "Do You Bore Yourself?" Happy thinkers never bore themselves because they always have a little happiness retreat that is colored with the exquisite hues of imagination and appreciation. And from this retreat lead paths of gladness that are open always to those who appreciate life, work, opportunity, and friends.

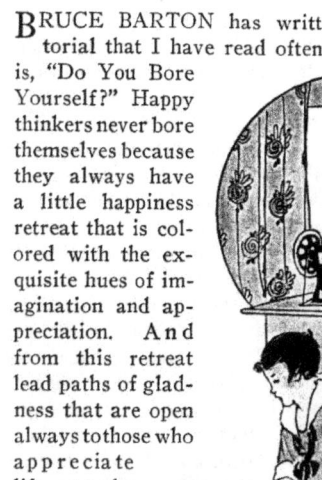

Two-Fabric Frocks

By ALWILDA FELLOWS
Department of Dressmaking

THE reign of high prices has been a trying period for the great majority of us, for it has required unusually careful planning to make every expenditure worth while and not of short, temporary value. But even such despotism as has been assumed by high prices has its advantages, for what could better inspire the designing of two-fabric styles, which permit the use of odd lengths of material, or the remodeling of dresses that have already given a season or two of servicce, by combining unworn sections taken from them with a yard or two of contrasting fabric?

And now that the two-fabric model has been found so satisfactory and pleasing in every respect, we shall be reluctant to discard it. It has taught us many a lesson in thrift simply because its very attractiveness and its use of comparatively small sections of material have suggested endless possibilities for utilizing every garment in our wardrobe, which may have become worn or somewhat out of date.

Hope for a decline in the price of materials has already had encouragement in the few cases where a favorable change has been made, and we have every reason to believe that the pinnacle of high prices has been surmounted. But even yet we should not pass by any opportunities for making the most of what we have on hand, for while fashion is favoring us with its recognition of two-fabric models, is the time to make use of every discarded garment that will lend itself to present use.

PERHAPS the prime favorite of the combination dresses is the type made of blue serge or tricotine and black satin. Not only is such a combination very pleasing as well as smart, but also it has a suggestion of utility that emphasizes its virtues.

Because of the popularity of this combination, a point that should receive special consideration in the planning of a dress of blue serge and black satin is the selection of a design that is unusual or the application of touches to disguise a style that might otherwise be duplicated many times. An example of a simple style that depends almost wholly upon its trimming for distinctiveness is shown in the model at the left. The main part of the dress is of serge, but because of the front panel and vest and the sleeve trimming bands of satin, almost any serge frock of rather plain and even scant design may be used to advantage in its development.

Heavy black silk floss embroidery with a touch of metallic thread forms a very pleasing border effect on the sleeve trimming bands, the panel, and the vest edges. The satin vest is parted toward the waist line to expose a vestee of very soft white silk, and the same silk is further evidenced in the collar. For some types, the use of a light color near the face is not really necessary, but for the majority of women such a touch seems to provide a softening tone that is essential.

PATTERN formation for a dress such as this is very simple. Use a plain-waist pattern for the foundation and, in cutting,

turn back the center front of the pattern to make provision for the vest effect. Cut the sleeves with the aid of a bell-sleeve pattern, and if the lower part of this pattern seems too wide, remove some of the width by laying in small darts from the lower edge.

Straight lengths of material, with or without seams at the center side, depending on the size of the pieces that must be employed, will prove suitable for the skirt if the dress is intended for an average figure. But if it is being made for a person that is large through the hips, the use of a plain skirt pattern that is slightly gored and has provision made for a little fulness through the waist and hip sections is advisable. Mark the panel on the pattern so that its full width will be about 15 inches at the lower edge and it will taper a trifle toward the waist line.

For the vest, provide two lengthwise strips of satin about 4½ inches wide and of a length that will prove becoming. Finish the center front and upper and lower edges with a bias binding of self-material that will be, when finished, about ¼ inch wide. After embroidering the vest, pin the sections to the waist, adjusting them so that they will meet at the neck edge and part several inches at the waist line. Then, at the center front, pin a strip of the light-colored silk, securing it underneath the dark-colored vest sections. Arrange the opening of the waist where the left side of the dark-colored vest section overlaps the lighter colored portion underneath, and the opening of the skirt on the seam line at the left side front.

A STYLE such as this would be lovely if made of a combination of satin with velvet, Georgette crêpe, or chiffon, or it might be made entirely of one kind of material with a little contrast afforded by the collar and inserted vest section. The back of the dress might be made very interesting by the addition of a panel extending from the shoulders to the lower edge of the skirt and looped under the hem.

WITH fall days approaching and indoor social activities beginning in earnest, sheer light dresses, although during the summer months they served appropriately for afternoon wear, do not seem quite suitable for indoor afternoon functions. And here the need of a dark silk dress is realized, for what is more disappointing than to feel the inadvisability of accepting an invitation simply because one's clothes do not seem well fitted for the occasion? It is really quite a simple matter to overcome such a disadvantage if one has just a little time to devote to remodeling, for, with a past season's dress and a yard or so of material that harmonizes with that in the dress, the identity of the older material may be completely disguised.

As an example of the possibilities in designing, note the dress shown at the right. A brown-satin dress made very plain in overblouse or short redingote effect with long, loose sleeves showed decided wear through the shoulders and upper part of the sleeves, although the remainder of the dress appeared only slightly soiled. A thorough cleaning renovated the unworn portions of satin, and the worn parts of the waist were replaced with a very soft silk having a deep tan background with figures that shaded into brown. The drop-shoulder effect was introduced as a means of entirely changing the blouse without discarding the lower sleeve portions, and sections cut from the lower portions of the waist were used to form a sort of connection between the waist and skirt of the new design. Then, as a means of lengthening the skirt portion of the overblouse, a deep band of the contrasting material was applied. Trimming of bound buttonholes and satin-covered buttons and a collar of ecru net completed a very attractive and strictly up-to-date costume.

Fall Millinery *Features*

By MARY MAHON
Department of Millinery

PERHAPS one of the most interesting turns in millinery this season is the elaborate use of ostrich, which, after a period of comparative neglect, promises to be a tremendous feature and bids well to remain throughout the winter. A change of trimming and embellishments is refreshing to style, and since our laws prohibit the wearing of aigrettes and we do not relish the constant use of imitation aigrettes very readily, our next resort is ostrich. So, after a careful survey of the new hats, it is quite evident that it is the feather plus unique treatment that lends charm to the hat beautiful.

Just now ordinary feather tips, that is, those having long flue feathers, have no special meaning when used in clusters. It is when they are separated and drenched or treated according to one of the many methods used at present to make the feather appear like something other than the original species, that you obtain the up-to-the-minute style touch.

FROM the small, flat palm-sized tip to the unbelievably long plumes produced through the artificer's skill, ostrich feathers are used on large and small hats. They droop over the edge of the brim or entirely cover the hat, and sometimes they hang down close to the right shoulder. This side-hanging trim is very pretty on small hats; not, however, on the very close, severe hats, which have the disadvantage of hardening the lines of the face and aging the wearer, but on hats with narrow brims that lend themselves to the newest trimming notes.

At present, no matter how small the hat may be, there must be some brim evident in order to obtain the new effect, and this suggestion of brim is gladly welcomed, for it is quite adaptable to the ostrich trim.

A modish way in which to pose the ostrich on such hats is to arrange it so that the curled tip falls downwards. Yet, in trimming large hats, many of the plumes are placed upstanding quite like in an old portrait effect, which, although centuries old, is ever new in beauty. However, in general, the whole tendency is toward the drooping effect in ostrich trimming.

RIBBON is the next important feature in today's millinery, and it certainly is put to odd uses. It seems quite certain that the solid ribbon hat will no longer be confined to sports hats alone, because many

smart models are made entirely of marvelous gold-brocaded ribbon, and velvet ribbon embroidered in elaborate designs is used for draping small turbans and, in many instances, for covering large-brimmed hats. In fact, ribbon of every width is used, from the narrowest baby velvet ribbon to the very widest, more stress being laid on the wide-width ribbons.

One effective French model recently seen was a basket-woven shape made of the tiniest velvet ribbon and having at the left side back a soft flowing artist's tie bow with loose ends hanging quite long. This bow was made of No. 60 satin ribbon. Such a combination of satin and velvet ribbon gives a decidedly unusual touch.

Ciré ribbon in black and negre brown is also employed in combination with the brocades for draping purposes. These pretty, soft-draped hats are popular at present and the ciré ribbon, because of its subtle softness, works well into graceful folds without adding weight to the hat. Also, as it has a close resemblance to leather, ciré can be used instead of kid, whose vogue is by no means ended.

SEVERAL of the new models are made of kid and trimmed in long ostrich quills of variegated coloring. When a light-weight hat is desired, ciré can be substituted for the kid without spoiling the effect.

Another smart leather hat is a little rolled-brim shape that is wide at the sides and developed in mocha tinted with dull gold. The leather is worked with the thread to give the appearance of scales. A handbag of the same material is decidedly unique.

A brown Chantilly lace veil is very effective over a medium-size hat when it is drawn to the right side and allowed to drop gracefully off the brim.

AS FAR as shapes go, it would seem that the important point is width from side to side. This silhouette continues in favor, and in some cases the wide side line is accentuated by trimming poked out beyond the brim edge.

Generosity in line is mentioned as one of the features in shapes for fall. But as the season advances and the large fur collars are worn, the large hat will be confined to evening wear. Then will come in evidence the softly draped tam effects deftly caught into a wonderful web of stitchery done in many colors bright enough to make the dullest wintry day appear warm and festive.

Our *First* Fashion Service

DURING the past month the Institute has been engaged in preparing for its full-paid and active dressmaking students a Fashion Service for the fall and winter season of 1920-21.

For a long time, it has been Mrs. Picken's desire to provide a Fashion Service with instruction especially for our students. Only recently was it possible for us to undertake so tremendous a task.

This Fashion Service, illustrating seventy-five variations of the season's best fashions and advanced styles in dresses, suits, coats, and wraps for all types of women, comes with definite information as to the construction of each garment. Such a book will bring happiness to every student entitled to receive it. In addition, it is an excellent example of the printing and engraving art.

This book, which will be issued in the future every fall and spring, is only another step forward in the service the Institute is constantly extending to its student body.

Our plans are to have the entire edition mailed by October 1. So if your account with us is in good standing, watch out for this Service, for it will prove a great help in planning your clothes for the coming season.

Salads in *Abundance*

By LAURA MacFARLANE
Editorial Department

WHILE we usually connect salads with the springtime of the year, it seems a little strange to do so when we consider the wealth of material that the early fall season offers. Practically every country home has a garden of its own which is yielding to the limit just now, and in the towns and cities fresh fruits and vegetables are to be had in great abundance in the markets. So, instead of trying to use these just as vegetables or as fruit in all of your meals, why not combine some of them into attractive salads?

SALAD ingredients usually consist of the food itself, such as fruit, vegetables, meat, fish, etc.; salad greens, such as lettuce, chicory, watercress, etc.; salad dressings, which improve the flavor of the salad; and salad garnishes, which are intended chiefly to appeal to the eye. Usually, there is a salad accompaniment, too, such as wafers of some kind, cheese sticks, and small dainty sandwiches.

SO FAR as the salad greens are concerned, they should be as fresh and crisp as it is possible to have them. Allow them to stand in the water 15 to 20 minutes. Then, lay the pieces on a dry towel, cup side down, so that they will drip, roll up the towel, and set in the ice box. Any leaves that are broken should not, of course, be discarded, for if they are in good condition, they can be shredded, that is, rolled up tight and then cut into narrow strips or shreds with a sharp knife.

IN PREPARING fruit for salad, have the pieces equal in size, similar in shape, and not too small. Oranges and grapefruit are used so frequently for salads that every one should understand their proper preparation. Peel these just like an apple, cutting the peeling deeply enough to remove the skin from the sections; then, with a sharp knife, cut out the contents of each section, passing the knife as closely to the skin as possible. They may be used in sections or cut up into pieces of any desired size. In the case of bananas, do not forget to scrape off the pithy surface, as this is disagreeable in a salad.

Nuts for salad should be chopped or cut, never ground, and they should be added to the salad just before it is served, as they have a tendency to darken the dressing and discolor an otherwise attractive salad.

SALAD garnishes, while not a necessity, form a very interesting part of this dish, for they give salads their psychological appeal, as important a point as the nutritive aspect of food preparation. Garnishes may consist of some highly flavored material, such as sweet pickles, olives, celery, a nasturtium leaf or flower; a material of contrasting color, as, hard-cooked egg, beet, tomato, pimiento, green or red pepper; radishes, plain or cut to resemble roses; a delicate material of some kind, as a tiny heart of lettuce or a tip of celery. Stuffed olives provide a good color contrast, and these are often sliced. Another attractive olive garnish is formed by paring an olive round and round the stone and thus producing a curl or spiral.

THERE are a number of salad dressings from which to choose. The personal preference of those to be served largely regulates the choice, but the variety of the salad has much to do with it. French dressing, which is used for the marinating of salads and as a dressing by itself, consists of 3 parts oil to 1 part vinegar and is seasoned with salt, pepper, paprika, and mustard. Mayonnaise dressing is preferred for meat and fish salads. Boiled salad dressing finds favor with those who do not care for oil.

Mayonnaise Dressing

½ tsp. salt 2 egg yolks
¼ tsp. pepper 1½ c. oil
¼ tsp. mustard 4 Tb. vinegar or lemon juice

Mix the dry ingredients in a bowl and add the egg yolks to them. Beat with a rotary egg beater until well mixed. Add a few drops of oil and beat. Add a drop of the vinegar or lemon juice, a few more drops of oil, and beat constantly. Gradually increase the quantity of oil added each time. Continue until all the oil and vinegar are used up, when the mixture will be thick and lemon-colored.

Boiled Dressing

2 Tb. butter 1 tsp. mustard
2 Tb. flour 1 c. milk
1 tsp. salt 2 eggs
2 tsp. sugar ⅔ c. vinegar

Melt the butter in the inner pan of a double boiler, add the flour, salt, sugar, mustard, and milk. Cook over the flame until thick. Beat the eggs, and stir in the vinegar, beating rapidly. Add the white sauce, return to the large pan of the double boiler, and allow to cook until the eggs have thickened. Cool and serve.

OF ALL the vegetables that this season offers, none is so versatile in the making of salads as the tomato. It makes a most appetizing salad when merely cut from the center in sections that are allowed to fall part way open on a bed of crisp lettuce leaves. Any of the dressings mentioned may be served on it in this form. Whole tomatoes and a few uncut string beans are sometimes combined in a salad. Tomatoes also form an important part of a combination salad in which the other vegetables may be sliced onions, sliced cucumbers, sliced peppers, and asparagus tips.

Again, tomatoes are often used as receptacles in which a salad mixture is placed. Select medium-sized, well-ripened tomatoes for such a salad, and hollow out some of the center so as to form shells. Fill these with any desired combination of vegetables or with a fish salad, such as crab meat, which should first be marinated, that is, mixed with French dressing or merely seasoned vinegar. Serve with mayonnaise as individual salads or place several of the stuffed tomatoes on a salad dish and serve at the table, adding the dressing here. This makes an excellent salad to serve with sandwiches or cheese sticks at an early fall luncheon or a Sunday night supper.

CUCUMBERS also lend themselves admirably to the preparation of salads. Every one is familiar with the small boat or hollowed out cucumber which makes a shell for a salad mixture consisting of diced tomatoes, celery, and cucumber. If a little variety in cucumber salad is desired, make cups of a different form by cutting cucumbers in half crosswise without peeling them and removing a slice from each end to make the receptacle stand evenly. Then with a small knife, remove the green rind in alternate strips until a green-and-white striped cylindrical cup is formed. This may be hollowed out and then filled with any appropriate salad. A good color scheme results when salmon salad is placed in such cups. The cucumber cups should not, of course, be eaten.

FRUIT salad continues to hold its own in this season of the year as well as in all others, for it cannot be exceeded in both appearance and flavor. Then, too, it offers so many possibilities both as to combination and decoration that one resorts to it again and again. Any of the dressings already given may be used on fruit salads or a sweet dressing may be made from fruit juices, such as pineapple, pear, orange, and lemon, sweetened a trifle, and thickened by means of eggs. This is allowed to cook in a double boiler until it becomes thick. If a good combination fruit salad is desired, grapefruit, oranges, bananas, apples, and pineapple may be used, but any one or more of these fruits may be omitted if they cannot be had. Cut the fruit into pieces the desired size, put together just before serving, and add the salad dressing. Serve on lettuce leaves and garnish with a few finely chopped nuts and maraschino cherries. A very attractive fruit salad can be had by arranging sections of grapefruit, orange, and canned peaches symmetrically on lettuce or romaine and garnishing it with a few red raspberries.

When cantaloups are at their best, it is a pretty fancy to serve fruit salad in halves of small cantaloups. Balls of the cantaloup cut with a French cutter form a very good garnish for such a salad. Or, if desired, an entire cantaloup salad can be had by placing pieces of the cantaloup pulp cut in any preferred form on lettuce or romaine and serving with a sweet salad dressing.

In a group of salads of all kinds seen a short time ago, the pear salad easily won first place because of its artistic effect. To make this salad, place half of a pear, canned or fresh, hollow side up, on a bed of lettuce and garnish with thick salad dressing, over which arrange several strips of pimiento. Halves of English walnut meats also make an effective garnish. If a salad having more food value is desired, add a ball of cottage or cream cheese to either pears or peaches.

With salads, probably more than with other dishes, the housewife has a chance to express her originality, for often the most artistic salads result when she follows her own ideas rather than definite recipes.

Woman's Institute *Question-Box*

A Dress for Mother

Some time ago when I was a beginner in dressmaking and had little confidence in my ability, you helped me with the selection of a style for a simple dress. I know that you will be pleased to hear that I was very successful in my first attempt to make a dress for myself. Since that time I have studied my individual type very carefully, and now I am not at all hesitant about relying upon my own ability in the selection of designs for myself. But my next problem is making clothes for mother. She has consented to let this be entirely a Woman's Institute dress; that is, I am to purchase the material, select the style, and complete the making and fitting with no help other than that of my lessons and suggestions you may give me. So again I'm taking advantage of your offer of assistance and I'll appreciate more than I can tell any help you may give me. Mother is of average height but rather stout, and with a very full bust. Her hair is gray and her complexion clear, although she has but little color.
S. R. E.

Mother problems are certainly interesting ones for us, as we delight in seeing mothers appropriately dressed and their charms enhanced rather than concealed.

This is an especially favorable season for the woman of generous proportions. The tendency for long lines with panels a leading feature is evident in all fall showings. Dark blue, brown, gray, and black, which, as you know, are very desirable for the stout woman, receive very special attention. And materials are really luxurious in their softness, being of just the texture and quality that are generally recommended as most suitable for advanced years and a well rounded-out figure.

For your mother, I suggest that you select very soft faille or satin in a dark, rich shade of blue or brown and embroider it in self-color silk floss with a touch of metallic thread. You may follow the general lines of the dress shown at the upper left, but change any details that you consider will make the style more becoming. Means of apparently decreasing the size of the bust are afforded by the vest and the collar, which is extended to the waist line. Also, the manner in which the collar is broadened at the shoulders draws attention to width at this point and thus directs it from the bust line. You may find it advisable, instead of making the vest entirely of self-material, to arrange surplice folds of the dark material in the lower part of the opening and similar folds of cream-colored net or chiffon for the upper part of the vest.

Give very special attention to the waistline finish. Make this quite loose and low so that the dress will fall comparatively straight and not appear pinched in at the waist line nor unfavorably emphasize the large bust.

Want to Get Acquainted?

The following Institute students desire to become acquainted with other Institute students residing in their localities:

Haines City, Fla.................................C. E. T.
East Smithfield, Pa............................M. R. N.
Middletown, Md.................................L. D.
Washington, D. C...............................C. E. S.
Paw Paw, Mich..................................K. M.
Meriden, Conn. ....D. D. S.
Virginia and North Carolina..............M. E. T.
San Diego, Calif................................F. W. J.
Bridgeport, Conn..............................M. E. McF.
Boston, Mass....................................M. B. T.
Bronx, N. Y......................................C. G.
Centralia, Wash................................G. M.
Danbury, Conn. ....M. E. N.
Charles City, Iowa............................E. B. A.
Hannaford, N. Dak............................J. B.
Edmonton, Alberta, Canada, and
   Wareham, Mass............................J. E. B.
Martin's Ferry, Ohio..........................M. R.
Jacksonville, Fla................................R. H. B.

I should like to become acquainted with a student of the Woman's Institute taking the Millinery Course who resides in Baltimore, Md.
G. S. S.

I should like to become acquainted with other Woman's Institute students taking the Complete Dressmaking Course who are about twenty years of age and live in Paterson, N. J.
M. V.

I should like to correspond with Woman's Institute students between the ages of 18 and 23 years.
E. B. G.

I should like to correspond with some girl between 15 and 20 years of age, taking the Woman's Institute Dressmaking Course.
F. B.

I should like to become acquainted with some student about 17 or 18 years of age, who is taking the Complete Dressmaking Course.
I. B.

I should like to become acquainted with a young married woman taking the Dressmaking and Tailoring Course who lives in the vicinity of Niles, or South Bend, Mich.
H. R. W.

I should like to correspond with other students between the ages of 16 and 19 who are taking the Dressmaking and Tailoring Course.
E. G.

I should like to correspond with a Woman's Institute student, taking the Dressmaking and Tailoring Course, who is 16 or 18 years of age, and living in Pennsylvania, or any other state.
P. M. B.

I should like to go into partnership with a first-class dressmaker in one of the California Coast towns, preferably southern or central coast. I could furnish all, or one-half, the money necessary to set up the business and would put in power machines.
J. A. T.

I should like to correspond with students, 17 years of age, in Canada or the United States.
J. E.

I should like to correspond with some one about 20 years old, taking the Complete Dressmaking Course.
R. B. C.

If other Woman's Institute students would like to get in touch with the inquiring students, we shall be glad to supply the addresses.

School Clothes

Vacation time was such a busy season for me that I seemed unable to find opportunity to make a new supply of school clothes for my little daughter. Now necessity demands that I take time for this work. Will you please give me a few suggestions as to practical materials and new methods of trimming?
A. C.

The ever-favored and very practical blue serge is worthy of the first consideration for school clothes. This year its principal trimming is wool embroidery, sometimes carried out in a bright color, red being especially good, and other times in a rather subdued or neutral tone, gray being quite popular.

Challis was favored to a certain degree last year, but this season it promises to enjoy the very height of popularity, for all the New York children's shops are featuring it in a very delightful way. Many of the challis patterns have a very dark background with bright colored flowers or figures, and they are trimmed with satin or grosgrain ribbon binding of a color to match the figure. For instance, black challis with tiny bright red flowers has not only a quaint charm but also a utility value of unusual degree.

For the very young school girl, a woolen dress, unless it is of a kind that will permit of frequent laundering, is not quite so satisfactory as little frocks of gingham, chambray, kindergarten cloth, and similar fabrics. Checked and plaid gingham dresses may rely almost wholly upon unusual features in the cut or the use of bias self-material for trimming. The plain materials offer possibilities for hand embroidery.

Our Students' Own Page

All the Hats She Wants

When Miss Catherine M. Harris, of Escanaba, Michigan, says in the accompanying letter that it seems like a dream to have all the hats she wants, we believe she is expressing the feeling of most women. But when, like Miss Harris, one can make one's hats at a saving of three-fourths of their cost in the stores, it is entirely possible to make that dream come true. Miss Harris writes:

Since I took up Millinery, I have made three hats and they are, if I may say, very becoming. Next week I intend to make two more. It seems like a dream to have all the hats you want, and besides I already have orders to make some hats for my friends, among them a wedding hat.

And I wish to say that I agree with the person who said, "The Course is worth more than the money." You can never know too much about such things as Millinery, Dressmaking, and Cooking.

Where the Money is Coming From

That is the problem which seems to have puzzled many of our members when they joined the Institute; but after a few lessons this problem usually solves itself. The experience of Mrs. O. C. Marteney, of Buckhannon, West Virginia, whose letter we are quoting here, illustrates how easily the money problem can be solved:

I find your Course of studies very interesting and helpful. I sewed some before taking the Course in home dressmaking. Every one I sew for seems to notice I am doing better work. I am much interested in sewing and have sewed to make all payments, and more than average eight to ten dollars a week and do the housework for my home.

Learns a Business at Forty-Nine

The theory that one cannot learn after passing a certain age has been exploded long ago. And it has been disproved by the experience of hundreds of our members who, well along in life, have proved that they *can* learn, and learn easily. The following letter from Mrs. Alice M. Hall, one of our members from up in Maine, shows what a woman in middle life can do, for Mrs. Hall was forty-nine when she joined the Institute. We'll let her tell her experience in her own words:

I was very anxious to see what I could do, and a year ago last spring I went to Boston and got a stock of millinery and turned my parlor into a millinery store. People were quite astonished when I came home with my hats. They said: "What does she know about millinery?" I soon showed them. Some woman said my show window was prettier than those of milliners who had been in business for years. Some said: "She bought her hats all ready trimmed; she never could do that work." But I kept right on—had fine success that spring, better in the fall, and have been growing all the time. I go away every season. This fall I went to New York, and so I have been very busy. I also use the customers' old material and make new hats for them out of it.

I would like you to see a turban I made today. It is a real feather turban. I think you would say I did well. I am so proud of my lessons that hundreds of dollars would not buy them. They are still my guide in millinery, and I refer to them very often. I find the colors and color combinations a great help to me.

Offered Fine Position Before Finishing Course

We received a very nice letter a short time ago from Mrs. Paul R. Heinrich, of Galveston, Texas, that reflects a great deal of credit on the fine work she is doing. Mrs. Heinrich writes:

I feel that I have done exceptionally well with my Millinery Course, and during the months of November and December I made twenty-five hats. Each one I made seemed prettier than the one before.

Although I have not finished my Course, one of the leading millinery shops here offered me a splendid position as milliner, but at the time I was unable to accept it.

Cooking Student Takes Prizes at County Fair

The practical value of our training in cookery is being especially appreciated just at this season when the prices of fruits and vegetables and the sugar to put them up are so high. Fortunate, indeed, is the woman who can do her canning and preserving with the supreme confidence that when she opens it next winter it will be as fresh and sweet as the day she put it away. You'll be interested in reading the following letter from Mrs. G. U. Healy, of Mineral Point, Wisconsin:

I have surely enjoyed these last two lessons on canning, preserving, etc., and found them of great value. I have a large assortment of fruits, jelly, and pickles for winter, and I did them from the directions in my lessons. I have had very few failures.

Perhaps you would be interested in knowing that I had first premium on sponge cake, currant jelly, and mixed candies at the fair here last fall, and I could not make the sponge cake or jelly before studying these lessons.

Finds a New Source of Power

Not the least important effect of successfully pursuing a course of study with the Institute is the new sense of power one feels through one's newly acquired accomplishment. For many of our members, the completion of one Course only opens their eyes to the wonderful possibilities for self-improvement that are tied up in their little odds and ends of time, and they quickly follow with the second and third Courses. This thought was very aptly brought out in the following letter we received recently from Mrs. G. E. Russell, of 191 Park Ave., Arlington, Massachusetts:

I never shall be thankful enough that I started my Course in Professional Dressmaking. As each new lesson comes, I am more delighted, and as I am nearing an end, I feel such a sense of power and independence, as well as ambition (for I shall not stop studying). I shall never cease being grateful to Mrs. Picken for all that she has done for me, nor shall I cease telling others about her and her work.

Saved $53 on One Garment

That it is easily possible to save the cost of a Course in one season is proved by hundreds of letters we receive. Here is one from Louise G. Zonner, of 31 Mulberry Street, Buffalo, N. Y., who saved almost the entire cost of her Course on a single garment:

This spring I made a Pekinese-blue wool velour dolman wrap for myself. The material, including lining, buttons, etc., cost $32. When I priced one similar to mine, they wanted $85 for it. Can you imagine how proud I was? It would take pages to tell all the things I have made.

SPECIAL NOTICE: For full information regarding Courses in Sewing, Dressmaking, Tailoring, Millinery, and Foods and Cookery as taught by the Woman's Institute, address all requests to the

WOMAN'S INSTITUTE OF DOMESTIC ARTS AND SCIENCES, Inc.
DEPT. 21, SCRANTON, PA.

Fashion Service
— SUPPLEMENT —

Each Issue of *Vintage Notions Monthly* includes a *Fashion Service Supplement*. You will read about the fashion styles popular in the early twentieth century and receive a collectible fashion illustration to print and frame.

The students of the Woman's Institute would also receive a publication called *Fashion Service*. Where the *Inspiration* newsletter instructed them on all aspects of the domestic arts, not only sewing but also cooking, housekeeping, decorating, etc., *Fashion Service* was devoted entirely to giving current fashions with a key to their development.

Fashion Service prided itself on providing it's readers with reliable style information and the newest fashion forecasting. The publication wasn't just eye candy. The Institute stressed the importance of studying the fashions to benefit the sewer's understanding of dressmaking. To quote founder Mary Brooks Picken, "Once the principles of design...and of construction… are understood, beautiful garments will result. This publication comes to you as an aid to this desired goal. Read the text of every page and reason out the why of every illustration and description that your comprehension of designing and construction may be enlarged and your appreciation made more acute."

Today, these articles and illustrations give us a historically accurate view of what fashion really meant 100 years ago. Not only can we study these articles for an "of-the-time" style snapshot, but just as their students did, we can also learn to understand the principles of design and increase our sewing skills. In each issue, look for a collectible illustration in the back of the supplement!

Winter Fashions

Down from the mountains, in from the fields and woods, we come, making our seasonal pilgrimage to Fashion's throne.

New York! Fifth Avenue! The fashion shows! The radiant windows! Then behind the scenes into the studios of the great designers.

And we come—for what? To learn what Fashion, here enthroned, decrees shall be the colors and the lines of dress for the impending season.

"Brown it shall be," we hear. "All the browns from the yellowish brown to the deeper, warmer tones. And red shall add its touch of brightness here and there, and there shall be glints of gold and silver."

And we stand a little in awe to think that out of mysterious studios tucked away in the teemingly busy buildings of a great hurrying city come these words of wisdom prophesying how milady shall deck herself for the Autumn promenade. It is awe of the genius of creative art.

But let one wiser speak than all the rest.

"You have come from the woods and the fields and the streams. Go back to them and you will find that whence you have come, there we have been to seek and choose the glories of your dress. The browns are of the spent and quiet fields that bore the Summer harvests, of the fluttering, falling leaves, with their glints of gold and flashes of red. The 'brick dust,' seeming new, is of the peaceful homes, gem-set among your smiling hills.

"Go back if you would find the source of all that Fashion decrees, and you will find it on Nature's own great canvas.

"In spring, she picks her colors from the nodding, wind-blown daffodil, from the budding, tender leaves of green, from all the pastel shades that lie on the petals of the first flowers.

"In autumn, from the brown and golden foliage and from the flushed red cheeks of ripened fruits.

"And so she will go on finding her inspiration always in the far-flung panorama of Nature herself, drawing each season a new and exquisite melody from the infinite tones of God's great instrument."

*W*HEN the curtain of style expectancy parted to reveal Fashion's newest triumph in dress creation, among the first models to appear was one that might have been inspired by anticipated beauties of very early fall. As shown at the lower right, the coloring of its waist portion, orange crêpe Roma with all-over gold embroidery in delicate vein work, and a touch of leaf green carried out in the sash and sleeve banding, give a marked suggestion of frost-brightened foliage. The black velvet skirt and mink banding are in tribute to winter fashion predictions.

Just above is a fall dance frock of black satin, its close basque softened with an exquisite lace bertha and its very full skirt overlaid at the center front with coral-colored ribbon panels suspended from lovely flowers of the same color.

Sufficiently versatile in character to complete an afternoon costume or to enfold the luxuriousness of an evening gown, the lovely wrap, as illustrated, is of toast and Mandalay duvetyn, embroidered over the lower side portions in honeycomb effect and collared in brown wolf.

Toast color is also the selection of the Canton crêpe dress with plaited panels, the panels on the skirt extending from triangular trimming motifs formed by interlaced strips of self-material.

Standing on Fashion's threshold, as if eagerly awaiting very formal mid-winter functions, the striking model of black chiffon velvet with surplice banding of spotless ermine is truly a regal interpretation of the 1922 draped mode.

Coat Dress

In some respects but little different from a model that was introduced a number of seasons ago and yet with style details so decisively of 1922 influence that it stands out as an entirely new design, the coat dress of the hour is an altogether appealing type.

And a very ambitious type the coat dress represents. Sometimes it assumes a slightly draped princesse effect with surplice wrap-around closing; other times it borrows from the Russian and appears with a low bloused waist line and a full-length side closing. Sometimes it chooses the least expensive of the woolens as its fabric; and again it shows no hesitancy in adopting the very richest velvet. But almost invariably serviceability is its dominant note.

The model illustrated is of navy Poiret twill having the front fashioned on princesse lines with a little of the length drawn up at the termination of the surplice closing and stitched in flat plaits. The cascade drapery is cut in one with the back skirt portion and permitted to fall over the side line of the one-piece front. An interesting feature is the manner in which the skirt material is drawn closely over the hips across the back in marked contrast to the gathered effects that have been favored for so long.

Black caracul edges the collar and sleeves, and just inside of the fur, Roman stripe ribbon contributes its bright coloring to enliven the general effect. A long, black-silk tassel is suspended from the side ornament.

Material and Pattern Requirements.—Provide 3¼ yards of material 54 inches wide, 1½ yards of fur banding, and the same amount of ribbon. If you wish, you may obtain a fabric trimming in imitation of caracul.

You may have difficulty in finding a pattern similar to this design, but if you obtain a surplice-closing, coat-dress style with one-piece back, you may cut the back portion at the waist line and form the skirt portion in developing the muslin model by using a straight length of material, letting one edge form the drapery.

Construction and Fitting.—Baste the various sections of the dress together, leaving the left under-arm seam open from the waist line to the lower edge.

In fitting the dress, observe the usual points that must be considered and then draw up the fulness at the side and pin in the plaits as illustrated. If the dress shows any tendency to fall to the front, lift it at the right-side waist line and pin a dart in the front portion, extending this from the under-arm line. This change will necessitate removing the basting of the under-arm seam below the waist line and repinning the seam.

After this first fitting, stitch the under-arm dart, if this was provided, and finish the seams.

Face the front upper corners of the dress to form the revers portions; then make the double collar, stitch its under portion to the neck line of the dress, and press open the seam. Next, baste the inside edge of the revers facings flat to the dress; then turn inside the free edge of the upper collar piece and baste it over the revers facings.

In the second fitting, pin the underlapping front waist portion to a facing strip or piece of very soft belting that may be hooked to a belting used across the back waist line. After noting that the collar, revers, and sleeves appear correct, pin the free edge of the one-piece front under the cascade effect. Also, pin a bias strip, cut about 4 inches wide, across the back waist line, making this as a soft crushed girdle.

Skirt Lengths.—After having completed the fitting of the dress, turn the hem at the lower edge.

This is another season when there is much difference of opinion expressed as to the matter of skirt lengths. It seems that the longer skirt sanctioned by Fashion for spring and summer received little general attention, even though it was adopted in Fashion centers. In these same Fashion centers, even longer skirts than those predicted last season are already being worn and are gradually being generally adopted; so it is certain that fall and winter modes all over the country will evidence considerably longer skirts.

For general wear, an 8- or a 9-inch length, according to individual becomingness, may be adopted; for afternoon dresses, a 6-inch length is better style; and for evening gowns, ankle length is noted in many designs.

Finishing.—Complete the dress by first slip-stitching the collar to the revers portion and covering the raw edges of the collar across the back neck line and the raw edges of the revers facings with a facing. Then face the fur strips and slip-stitch these, as well as the ribbon, to the collar and sleeves. Also, slip-stitch the back girdle portion to the dress. Have the edge of the cascade drapery picoted so that the finish will not be heavy, and tack the underlapping skirt edge just back of the cascade.

Turbans Feature Vizor Brims

Shapes, particularly those of the turban variety, show a strong inclination toward the modified vizor brim. Sometimes, the vizor effect is gained by a crush of the material, and again by a bulgy ridge in the frame.

In Model 1, the narrow vizor is rounded out instead of defined, the manner in which the material is applied accomplishing this feat. A tam frame, shaped very low at the right side and high on the left side, is used for the foundation. Navy Lyons velvet, 1⅛ yards long and shirred in rows along the length of the material, the rows of shirring being run 1 inch apart, is draped over the foundation frame. Beginning at the right side, the material is laid easy around the frame, drawn into the head-size, and then shaped in soft folds so as not to define the outline of the frame, but to produce a cup effect at the center top.

A variegated ostrich fancy, repeating the colors of the Roman striped ribbon that trims the dress, is attached at the right side.

Model 1

Vintage Notions Monthly ©2016 Amy Barickman, LLC

Variations of Coat Dress

Model 1A.—A lovelier and more serviceable afternoon costume than this model would be difficult to find, for its material, color, trimming, and design are all of versatile character, being sufficiently conservative for street wear and yet lovely enough to grace an afternoon function.

Velvet in Mandalay brown, which is a rather deep tone, provides a harmonizing background for the fur that edges the full-length side-front closing, the bateau neck line, and the sleeves. The embroidery on the sleeves is of wool, being in soft tones of green, gold, and blue, colors that are repeated in the ornament at the side-front waist line. A sash of the velvet extends from underneath this ornament across the back waist line and at the right side is formed into a loop and the long end that is left hanging is finished with a tassel.

Average material requirements for this design include about 4 yards of velvet, 3¼ yards of narrow fur banding, and 4 small skeins of yarn.

A point to keep in mind when working with velvet is that the various portions of the dress must be cut so that the nap runs in the same direction in all, for two sections having the nap running in opposite directions will appear as two distinct tones, the deep shading of the velvet causing this. Opinions differ as to whether the nap should run up or down in the finished garment. Velvet appears richer and with greater depth of coloring when the nap runs up; also, it does not become flattened so quickly across the back skirt portion when it is cut in this manner. Chiffon velvet or any velvet that is pressed should be cut the same as broadcloth, that is, with the nap running down.

Model 1B.—Providing tucks in abundance is one of Fashion's ways of adding smartness to a costume this season. In this model they cover the entire skirt portion, which is attached at the hip line to a surplice waist having decidedly tailored tendencies.

The advantage of the hip-line seam is that it permits a straight section and an even hem line in the skirt, even though the side closing is laid in plaits near the waist line. Then, too, this seam appears as a pin tuck and therefore does not mar the design in the least.

A novel cut characterizes the sleeve, which is of a type that promises to become very popular. This is close fitting at the armhole, but gives evidence of a flare from the elbow to within about 3 inches of the wrist, where enough of the width is taken out to make the wrist edge close-fitting. The little cuff effect thus formed is decorated with pin tucks to carry out the skirt trimming, and small self-covered buttons are sewed over the seam line that joins the cuff edges at the back. Larger self-covered buttons and braid loops provide a means of fastening at the waist-line closing.

Broadcloth in tiffin, which is a dark shade of toast, is the material of which the frock is developed, 3 yards of this material being required for the average figure.

Model 1C.—Plaid novelty woolen of homespun weave, although an inexpensive material, adds a great deal of interest to this one-piece coat dress. The predominating color of the fabric is Royal blue, one of the bright tones that seem very promising for fall. This color is subdued a trifle by the plaid, which is carried out in gray, but appears without modification in the plain material of which the skirt trimming band, the narrow sash, the covered buttons and bound buttonholes, and the sleeve facings are made.

Darts at the front armhole and several inches below the waist line make possible a straight line at the lower edge, a point of merit when plaid is being used. They also permit a means of fitting a well-rounded figure, but for such a type, plain material should be substituted for the plaid; otherwise, the design with its long lines is very good for a generously proportioned person.

As illustrated, the collar is cut on the bias and a bias strip is used for trimming the sleeves.

For the average figure, provide 3 yards or more of material 54-inches wide, the amount depending on the size of the plaid, as allowance must be made for the matching of the plaids. Of plain material 54 inches wide, ¼ yard will be sufficient.

Model 1D.—Bonfire red, a color that is delightful in contrast with dark hair and eyes, is used unstintedly in this Canton crêpe model. And no attempt is made to provide a subduing influence, even in the braid trimming, for this evidences a dominating note of matching red with a bit of green and gold combined for effective contrast.

This coat dress is in two-piece bloused effect, which sets it definitely apart from the general run of coat-dress styles.

Novelty is especially evident in the sleeves and collar, the sleeves being of kimono cut and very wide and baggy at the under arm, and the collar applied to a broad neck line in upstanding effect, a bit trying for some types, it must be admitted, but very chic and charming for the youthful person having well-rounded, but not decidedly plump, features.

The pockets, one of which is merely simulated, are in stand fashion, and by their arrangement provide an effect that balances well with the side closing trimmed with double rows of braid.

Material requirements for the average figure include about 4 yards 40 inches wide and 7 yards of braid.

In cutting the blouse portion from material 40 inches wide, it will be necessary to supply piecings for the sleeve portions, which may be applied so as to give the effect of a very deep drop-shoulder line, as shown. If the style is being cut from 54-inch material, however, the entire blouse portion, including the sleeves, may be cut in one piece. Only the very softest woolens and those lightest in weight are suitable for a design that has as much fulness at the underarm as this.

1A 1B 1C 1D

Straight-Line Dress

A certain indication of popular approval attends Fashion's sanctioning of one type of costume season after season, for just as surely as Fashion introduces any design that is not generally becoming and does not combine with the comfort-giving qualities that are consistent with modern ideas, the style is doomed to short duration.

Variously known as the one-piece or, in its simpler form, the chemise type, the straight-line dress is one that has withstood the test of popular favor and comes to us again this season, unchanged in its general style but with details so new and charming that, on first appearance, it might pass as a decided change in design.

Not an ordinary note can be found in this straight-line model of navy Poiret twill. The broad kimono sleeves and the pointed side skirt sections are perhaps the newest features in the cut, and these, being embroidered in all-over lattice effect with gray wool and ornamented with appliqué motifs of duvetyn, are pleasingly emphasized. But the wide front and back panels receive a generous bit of attention, also, for these are pin-tucked in close rows, a treatment that is almost certain to become one of the most popular of the season.

To the person of average or generous proportions, this model would lend becoming lines, but it would serve only to accentuate the height and slenderness of the tall, angular type. With a fitted armhole and the embroidery omitted, the design would be suitable for the stout woman.

Material and Pattern Requirements.—Provide about 3 yards of material 54 inches wide for making this dress for the average figure. For the appliqué motifs, about ¼ yard of duvetyn will be needed and for the embroidery, about 12 small skeins of floss.

Use a one-piece pattern having kimono sleeves and full-length front and back panels or, in developing a muslin model, mark the panel lines and provide for the pointed effect on the side sections of the skirt. In order to avoid a seam through the center of the pointed end, the side skirt section might be made of a straight piece and joined to the sleeve and side body portion at the waist line, rather than cut in one with it.

It will be well to mark the embroidery design on the muslin model so as to gain an idea of its effect before applying it to the dress material.

Construction and Fitting.—Before cutting the front and back panels, pin-tuck the material, being very careful to space the tucks accurately and to make them as tiny and even in width as possible. Tuck only as much material as is needed for the panels, leaving an untucked space at each side for a finish at the outer edge. In cutting, allow merely a wide seam at the bottom.

In preparation for the first fitting, merely baste the under-arm seams and then baste the side skirt sections to the sleeve and side body portions, provided they have been cut separately, and the panels to the side portions.

In the first fitting, observe the manner in which the dress hangs, and decide whether the effect could be improved by a slight alteration in the width of the panels or in the bagginess at the under arm. Do not make the mistake of fitting closely, however, for this might detract from the style value without adding to the becomingness of the design.

After stitching and pressing open the under-arm seams, join the separate skirt sections, if they have been provided, by adjusting any fulness they may have over the waist line of the sleeve and side body portion, stitching them together and covering the raw edge with a narrow bias facing of self-material. Join the panels by turning under the edge and stitching them flat to the side sections, just inside of the turned edge so as to simulate a pin tuck.

Make the belt double so that it is about 1 inch wide when finished and long enough to confine the dress but slightly at a low waist line.

At this stage, try on the dress, observe whether the sleeve and neck lines are correct, pin the ends of the belt to the buckle, and place this around the figure, adjusting the length as you desire. Then turn the lower edge of the skirt, keeping the line even across the front and back and shaping the pointed sides in an attractive manner.

Finishing.—Apply the embroidery and the appliqué motifs, following the design illustrated or some other plan of decoration.

Finish the neck line with a narrow bias facing and the sleeves with a wide facing of self-material or of material like that used for the appliqué motifs. Also, face the lower edge of the skirt, using self-material or silk of a matching color and shaping either a straight or a bias piece the same as the lower edge of the skirt, making it broad at the side to include the pointed portions.

Unusual Diversity in Cushion Brims

A combination of black ciré satin and silver antique developed over a vizor-brim turban frame makes this cushion-brim hat of unusual distinction.

For the pattern of the cushion brim, cut an oval-shaped head-size in an oblong piece of paper 17 inches by 20 inches, the 20 inches indicating the width from side to side. After this, measure off the width of the brim as described in Art. 4, *Solid Foundations*, the back and front being 4½ inches; the sides, 6¼ inches; and the diagonal points, 5¼ inches.

With this pattern cut one layer of satin, one of silver cloth, and two of crinoline. Machine stitch these together around the outer edge, turn right side out, and steam the edge flat. Next, apply it to the frame with the satin for the facing and the silver cloth for the top brim, stitch secure to the head-size, and attach a balloon crown of the satin. To form the dented flare at the left side, shape the front portion up toward the crown, in close across the back, and down at the right side.

A flat loop of the satin, caught with a silver button to the right side crown, serves as trimming and extends a trifle beyond the brim edge.

Model 2

Variations of Straight-Line Dress

Model 2A.—One of the very commendable features of this straight-line model of navy twill is the simplicity of its cut, and yet the design is not at all ordinary.

An inserted front panel of rose duvetyn extending hip depth into the skirt portion is partly responsible for the individuality of the design, but most of the credit must be given to the arrangement of the black novelty braid. Besides outlining the panel effect, it is applied at each side front and side back in lines extending from the lower edge of the skirt to 6 or 8 inches above the waist line; also, it edges the sleeves and extends in double rows for 4 or 5 inches along the center. Black silk embroidery covers the joining of the lower edge of the duvetyn to the twill. The ends of the braid belt are clasped at the side front with a novelty buckle.

Of material 54 inches wide, provide 2½ yards for the average figure with ¾ yard of duvetyn, 7½ yards of braid, and 1 skein of floss for trimming.

The pattern suggested for use in the cutting of this model has a vest portion that terminates above the waist line. Determine, by placing the pattern over the figure, how far you desire the contrasting material to extend into the skirt and then extend the pattern lines of the vest.

Model 2B.—Since matelassé is accorded such a prominent position among the season's fabrics, it seems but right to let the design in which it is developed be subordinate to it, as in this model having Java, a medium brown, matelassé as its principal fabric. The full-length side closing, the lower edge of the skirt, and the neck are edged with Canton crêpe of a matching color, and the sleeves are trimmed with a band of the same material. The braided girdle of the crêpe, fastened with a fabric rose, gives a soft finish that detracts from the severity of the design.

For a very serviceable and comparatively inexpensive dress, this design suggests development in wool crêpe with trimming of crêpe de Chine of a harmonizing color.

Material requirements for the average figure include 3¾ yards, 40 inches wide, with 1½ yards for trimming, provided a piecing is made at the waist line.

Model 2C.—A lower sleeve portion of contrasting color joined in rather eccentric fashion and straight strips of this same material applied to provide interest at the side of the skirt, which is the custom nowadays, may lend all the variety that is needed in a design, as this model illustrates.

Canton crêpe is the material employed, black as the major color and comet blue, which is a soft, medium tone, for the contrasting portions. Embroidery in black silk floss follows a sketchy design on the contrasting color.

A model as simple as this is becoming to the majority of types, for it may be made as a one-piece or as a blouse style, and besides, it is a very practical sort of costume as it might be worn on many different occasions.

Provide 3½ yards of material 40 inches wide with 1 yard of contrasting color and 6 skeins of floss for the average figure.

In developing a sleeve of this kind, first cut a muslin model with the aid of a flared pattern and mark on this the pointed outline. After the muslin is cut on the marked line, the separate sections may be used for cutting the contrasting material. Then, to provide a soft effect at the joining line of the two sections, first finish the pointed edge of the upper sleeve with a fitted facing and then slip-stitch the lower sleeve portion close to this.

Make the skirt as a plain gathered model and supply a separate full-length front portion for an apron effect, edging this with the contrasting color.

Model 2D.—One way of drawing attention from an inexpensive woolen is to employ embroidery rather lavishly, as in this model, over much of the surface that would otherwise bear closest scrutiny. Not that such material justifies the expenditure of tedious hours of labor, however, for a heavy floss, such as stitchette or ribbonzine, applied in a simple darning-stitch can be worked up very effectively in just a short time.

In this instance, navy twill is embroidered with black ribbonzine over much of the front waist portions and over the upper portion of the sleeves. The design, with its narrow inserted front panel and applied side panels, would prove suitable for a generously proportioned figure, if the neck line were shaped for individual becomingness.

For the average figure, 3 yards of material 54 inches wide and 6 skeins of floss are needed, with 1 yard of silk for facing the panels.

Model 2E.—Groups of pin tucks extending the full length of each under-arm seam, an applied skirt drapery, and narrow collar and cuffs in scalloped outline overlying scalloped strips of duvetyn in contrasting color are the distinguishing features of this Kasha cloth model. Developed in navy with trimming of red, it would be very lovely, or in a colorful tan with trimming of brick-dust, perhaps a bit more unusual.

Any of the soft woolen or heavy silk fabrics are suitable for this design; also, in place of the duvetyn, crêpe de Chine or Canton crêpe might be used as trimming.

As a rule, 2¾ yards of material 54 inches wide is ample for a model such as this. For trimming, ⅛ yard of duvetyn is needed.

You may cut the dress with the aid of a one-piece pattern and in making it insert a triangular piece of material to provide the cascade drapery at the left side. Cut this triangular section so that it measures about 14 inches along a crosswise edge and almost ¾ yard along a lengthwise edge, and insert the bias edge in the seam, tapering this to make it of the required skirt length.

Have the edges of the drapery, the collar and cuffs, and their underlying trimming pieces picoted.

Vintage Notions Monthly   ©2016 Amy Barickman, LLC

Blouse Dress

When one is of very slender build, the blouse dress is the safest selection of style that can be made, for its generous fulness and soft waist-line finish serve to conceal lines that seem to follow an angular rather than a curved silhouette. Besides, blouse dresses are usually characterized by crosswise lines, which tend to direct attention to apparent width, in contrast with straight-line dresses whose purpose is to emphasize height.

Blouse dresses are generally of the two-piece variety, having the waist and skirt cut separately and the blouse formed by means of a waist lining cut shorter than the outside portion and secured to it at a low, loose-fitting waist line or by an elastic run through a waist-line casing, a method that permits the waist line to be raised or lowered at will. In the case of the model illustrated, a waist-line casing, which permits the dress to be slipped over the head, is essential, for the opening extends only part way down the center back.

This model gives an idea of the hold of crepe on popular favor and of the distinction it is possible to achieve by using nothing other than self-material for trimming, for the entire costume is of Canton crêpe, gray and black in combination. The seam that joins the two colors in the kimono blouse is covered with flat rosettes formed of narrow bias strips of material. A strap of the material extends from the abbreviated sleeve and is held in a rather wide but close-fitting wrist band. The skirt has a wide band of the gray edged with rosettes and is overlaid with narrow side panels.

Material and Pattern Requirements.—For the average figure, 3 yards of black crêpe, 1⅜ yards of gray, and 1 yard of chiffon for facing the panels are needed.

Form a muslin model for the waist, cutting it with the aid of a kimono waist pattern, and with the muslin model on the figure, mark a line for the joining of the contrasting materials. Then cut the muslin on the marked line and use the sections thus formed in cutting out the waist. Make allowance for a center-back closing in the upper portion, but cut the lower portion with the center back on a fold.

Use simply straight lengths for the skirt or shape them with the aid of a slightly full two-piece pattern. Cut the skirt band of contrasting material 10 to 12 inches wide, strips for the sleeve bands 5 or 6 inches wide and long enough to loop in the manner illustrated, and pieces for the wrist bands of this same width and equal in length to the hand measurement. For the side skirt panels, cut strips about 12 inches wide and round the lower corners as illustrated.

Construction and Fitting.—Turn and baste hems at the center back of the upper waist portion; then baste the sections of the waist together. Before stitching, take care of any fitting that may be necessary; then stitch the waist sections together, first stitching the crosswise seams and then finishing them on the wrong side as narrow flat fells secured with tiny hemming-stitches. Finish the under-arm edges in French seams.

Next, join the upper and lower skirt portions as suggested for a similar joining in the blouse; then stitch the side seams and press them open, finish the lower edge with a tiny hem or binding, and gather the waist line.

In preparation for the fitting, face the panels; also, make the sleeve straps and wrist bands double, as you would a narrow belt.

In the fitting, first tie a tape around a low waist line to restrain the fulness of the waist, blouse the waist as much as you desire, and adjust the fulness properly. Then pin the skirt to the waist, hanging this from the waist line if the length needs adjusting, and pin the panels in position. Also, pin the sleeve straps in place.

Finishing.—Take out the gathering in the skirt, keeping the pins adjusted properly, sew the waist, skirt, and panels together flat, forming a casing, and run an elastic through it, taking care to make this long enough to give a loose effect at the waist line.

Face the neck and sleeve edges and finish the edges of the wrist band separately so that they may be snapped together. Make the sash double so that it will be about 1 inch wide when finished, and tack this merely at one under-arm seam.

Form the rosettes over circular pieces of material picoted or hemmed on the edges. Determine the size for these pieces by dividing the length of the seam line over which they are to be applied by the number of medallions you desire. Cut the bias strips for the rosettes about 1½ inches wide; then, folding the strip lengthwise through the center, start applying it around the outer edge and work toward the center, letting the folded edge cover the stitches used to secure the preceding row. Attach the rosettes by merely tacking them in position.

Style Tempered with Good Taste

The combining of black and gray in Model 3 is a true indication that style is here tempered with good taste, because the elegance of the fabric, coupled with the simplicity of trimming and color tone, produces an unusually lovely hat.

The medium-size, soft-rolling brim, having a modified point in front and slashed at the right side to give the tricorne effect, is covered plain with black hatters' plush and finished with a corded edge.

The semi-bell crown has its top covered plain with the hatters' plush, and a bias strip of it is draped in soft folds for the side crown and finished around the top edge with a heavy cord.

A fancy spray of metallized burnt peacock, which is attached to the base of the crown at the right side over the slash, is allowed to droop in a scintillating shower of variegated silver tones that are pleasing in effect and give the correct rhythm to the costume.

Model 3

Variations of Blouse Dress

Model 3A.—Slip-over models have proved such a convenience and are so very practical that even many of the blouse dresses are cut in one-piece fashion and made with an elastic restraining the waist-line fulness or with separate waist and skirt portions joined in such a manner as to form a casing for an elastic. Either plan of cutting is permissible for this model, which has an opening at the center back just long enough to permit the dress to be slipped over the head with ease.

Black Kasha is the material of which the dress is made, while the trimming is of bright blue. In parallel rows of braid, this color is applied to the narrow, full-length side panel, the sleeves, and the belt, and in motif effect above and below the waist line at each side back. In embroidery, the color breaks the long lines of the waist and appears again in the sleeve, a Chinese design being carried out in couch-stitching.

Provide, for the average figure, about $2\frac{1}{2}$ yards of 54-inch material, 5 skeins of floss, and 22 yards or more of braid if this is to be applied in groups of five rows.

Model 3B.—Looking back over Fashion's pages is bound to impress one with the favor that has been accorded blue-and-gray combinations, for hardly a season has passed for several years without recognition of the possibilities of blue and gray. Fortunately, this season is no exception, and so we have lovely soft-toned models, such as the one shown here, to satisfy those who prefer them to the brighter colors.

Heavy silk crêpe is the blue material employed, while gray crêpe of lighter weight provides the narrow vest, the turn-over portion of the high collar, and the band at the lower edge. Novel treatment is evident in the embroidery of blue silk floss, which extends over several rows of silver stitching near the gray crêpe. Small filigree buttons extend part way down the center front and along the back of the sleeve.

According to accounts of Parisian openings, this type a sleeve, tapering from a very broad armhole to a tight wrist edge, is one that is especially worthy of note.

Average material requirements include $3\frac{3}{4}$ yards of 40-inch material, $\frac{1}{2}$ yard for trimming, 4 skeins of blue floss, and 6 small skeins of silver.

Model 3C.—Elegant simplicity seems to be just the right description for this model, in which brocaded silk crêpe in a lovely gray verging on tan combines with mole banding for sleeve, neck-line, and waist-line adornment. The use of fur as a girdle is very unusual, but it cannot fail to please on a figure that is slender and youthful.

Novelty of design is afforded by the sleeves, which fall in deep panel effect below the elbows, and side skirt panels, which are looped to make a portion of them double. Experiment with muslin to form a pattern for these skirt panels, observing that the full-length portion of the panel on the left side of the dress forms the under part, while just the reverse arrangement is true on the right side, where the shorter portion is underneath.

To develop the dress, as illustrated, for the average figure, provide $5\frac{1}{4}$ yards of silk, $1\frac{1}{2}$ yards of narrow fur banding, $1\frac{1}{4}$ yards of wider fur banding, and $\frac{1}{4}$ yard of lace for the shallow yoke.

Model 3D.—This Canton crêpe model of Lanvin green, which is similar to reseda, relies on the newness of its color for much of its distinction, and yet the design is one that evidences smartness in every detail. The waist is cut in surplice fashion and has kimono sleeves, which are joined at the elbow to deep cuffs having a decided flare. The front apron effect has fulness concentrated at the sides and seemingly held by the ornaments used on the girdle, which is formed of corded shirrings. At the left side, the apron is extended and permitted to fall in a cascade drapery, while at the right side it is extended just beyond the side seam line of the skirt and finished with a straight edge.

In the development of this model, about 5 yards of material 40 inches wide and a piece of lace for the vestee, if this is desired, will be needed.

Model 3E.—Trelaine, one of the aristocrats of the family of knitted woolens, is very desirable for models such as this, which are not of intricate cut. Navy is the chosen color, in this instance, with collar, vestee, lower sleeve portions, and trimming pieces on the waist of Canton crêpe in a pure medium red, dignified this season by the name of salvia.

The decoration of the contrasting color is unusual, consisting of embroidery in red floss worked around flat white bone and red wooden beads. Only one skirt panel is deemed necessary, this being secured in line with the trimming piece on the waist.

In developing this model for the average figure, provide 4 yards of material 40 inches wide with $\frac{3}{4}$ yard 40 inches wide for trimming.

Model 3F.—Crêpe Roma, that sheer, lovely fabric, chooses tiffin, a bright but rather deep tan, as an excellent color to use in combination with dark blonde lace in this design. No stinting is evident so far as the lace is concerned, for it is used to form an entire underskirt as well as the blouse.

The crêpe Roma overskirt is in three pieces, a center-back panel and slashed side sections that extend from the center front to the side back. All the edges of the overskirt are finished with bindings of self-material. The yoke arrangement, also, is formed of strips of self-material interlaced at the shoulder; and wider strips of the material falling carelessly over the arm give a tantalizing semblance of a sleeve.

For the average figure, $2\frac{1}{2}$ yards of crêpe and 3 yards of lace are needed for a model such as this.

Vintage Notions Monthly ©2016 Amy Barickman, LLC

Circular-Tendency Dress

A season without rumors of an approaching vogue for circular skirts has been indeed a rarity for some time. Each spring and fall, one or more ambitious designers have included the circular mode in their showings, perhaps as "feelers" to try out public opinion in regard to so pronounced a style change. And almost always the circular mode was adopted by so few that it was forgotten before another season rolled around. According to all reports, however, designers now feel that the public is warming up to the circular movement, as the French call it, for a fall showing that does not include evidences of the circular tendency is the exception rather than the rule.

There is a great deal of leniency, though, in the manner in which this circular movement is achieved, and some of the varieties are so thoroughly practical and may be so easily developed that even the staunchest supporter of the straight silhouette cannot help but be won over to them.

First of all, there is the type of skirt having an all-round flare. Then another has most of the flare concentrated at the sides. In many cases, the flare is not in the skirt itself, but instead, an apron section, side panels, or draperies of circular cut are poised over a foundation skirt and thus give the flared silhouette.

An all-around flare characterizes the youthful model that is illustrated, and black chiffon velvet, the fabric of which the dress is made, enhances the beauty of the rippled effect as no other material could. The elaborate embroidery, which is carried out on the skirt alone, is of heavy Royal blue floss combined with metallic silver thread. Still another note of interest in the skirt is the manner in which the waist-line fulness is concentrated in rows of shirring at the sides.

As for the basque waist, it seems satisfied to let its slender simplicity emphasize the charm of the skirt, although it does strive for original expression by means of an opening cut over the upper arm and a long puffed sleeve of Royal blue chiffon. The "seaman's rope" girdle at the low waist line, also of the chiffon, is a trimming that is receiving much well-deserved attention this season.

Material and Pattern Requirements. — For the average figure, about 4 yards of velvet, 1½ yards of chiffon, 15 skeins of heavy silk, and 6 small skeins of silver thread are needed to develop this model with a circular skirt of medium width.

For cutting out the dress, use a semi-fitted basque pattern, with bateau neck line and drop-shoulder effect and a circular skirt pattern having side waist-line fulness.

In cutting the skirt, you may find it necessary to apply side piecings if you use a two-piece pattern. To avoid such piecings, you may divide the pattern into three sections, providing a seam at the center back and moving the side seam farther toward the front, or make side-front and side-back seam lines and omit the center-side seams. Do not allow for a hem, as the skirt should be faced.

Construction and Fitting.—After basting the hems at the center back and the under-arm seams, fit the waist if necessary, but do not shape the under-arm lines decidedly. Then whip the hems at the center back and stitch and steam open the under-arm seams. Join the sleeve edges with French seams, gather the lower edge, and apply the wrist bands. Also, stitch the skirt seams, and supply the shirring at the sides.

In the second fitting, pin the skirt over the lower edge of the waist, drawing up and adjusting the skirt fulness at the sides. Then pin in the sleeves and note the neck line. Last of all, turn an even line at the lower edge of the skirt, being careful to let the folds hang perfectly free and not to pull down the material as you measure the distance from the floor.

Finishing.—In finishing the dress, face the lower edge of the skirt with light-weight silk that matches the dress in color. Also, face the neck, the edges of the opening over the upper arm, and the joining of the waist and skirt with narrow strips of bias silk, and secure the shirrings to stay pieces of silk placed underneath. After stitching in the sleeve, finish the armhole by turning under the edge of the sleeve portion and whipping it flat to the waist.

Instead of attempting to mark the embroidery design on the skirt, place the paper pattern over the skirt, work over this through the skirt, and then tear the paper away.

For the "seaman's rope" girdle, use a foundation of thick, soft cording; cover this loosely with chiffon and over the covered cording, place another seamed covering of the chiffon made considerably wider than the foundation covering. Twist the chiffon so as to give the effect that is illustrated, taking care to cover the seam with a fold. After joining the ends to form a circle of the measurement needed, secure the girdle in position with slip-stitching.

Chiffon Velvet as a Hat Fabric

Chiffon velvet, returning after a long absence as a hat fabric, is admirably suited for developing the irregular-brimmed hat shown on Model 4. Fitted severely plain with the velvet, the easy-rolled, long-front brim tapers down at the left side and shapes up close to the crown at the right side back, supplying a vantage point for the trimming. Like the brim, the top of the crown is covered plain and a bias strip of the velvet is drawn in soft folds around the side crown to the right side back.

For trimming, a bias strip of the velvet, 7 inches wide and 40 inches long, is made into a one-loop and two-end bow. This bow is attached at the right side back, the loop extending across the back into a rather high point at the left side. The two pointed ends, which have first been faced with Royal blue, shot-silver metal cloth, extend beyond the brim at the right side, thus accentuating the width across the back.

For this model, 1 yard of velvet 36 inches wide and ¾ yard of silver cloth will be required.

Model 4

Variations of Circular-Tendency Dress

Model 4A.—A front apron effect provides circular influence in the skirt of this model of navy serge, and the flare is repeated in the very wide cuffs, which join the close-fitting sleeves at the elbow. Of more than passing interest is the arrangement of the narrow silk braid applied in triple rows around the sides and waist line of the apron and around the lower edge of the waist, thus forming a wide band across the front waist line, which is copied in the treatment of the cuffs.

Taken as a whole, the style is rather severe, but if worn by a slender, youthful type of average height it might boast an enviable smartness that is not easily achieved.

Of material 54 inches wide, 3¼ yards will be required for the average figure. If the braid is applied as shown, about 15 yards will be needed.

In fitting the waist portion of this style, do not shape the under-arm lines very decidedly. Simply curve them in enough to give a semifitted effect, and keep the low waist line sufficiently loose to permit the lines of the dress to fall gracefully.

Model 4B.—It would be difficult to overestimate the attractiveness and usefulness of the novelty girdles of this season. They are made in such unusual designs and delightful colorings and are suitable for so many purposes that they are especially deserving of the prominent position they hold among trimmings.

Since the all-black costume has loosed its hold on popular favor, the novelty girdle has proved its worth in providing the essential touch of color, for this almost invariably lends a smart effect, while other means of adding color, unless carefully worked out, do not insure so much satisfaction.

A fancy jade girdle provides the color note in this model of black fancy crêpe satin and Canton crêpe. Here the inserted sections, godet-like in character, in the sides of the plain skirt, give the circular tendency and at the same time concentrate fulness at the sides. As is the case with many of the inserted side pieces, the length is made considerably greater at the center than where they join the front and back sections. The lower sleeve portions, although made full length, are slashed at the back and therefore provide but little protection for the arm.

Average material requirements include 2¼ yards of fancy silk and 2¼ yards of plain.

Model 4C.—The soft, shimmering surface of crêpe satin adds much to the charm of a circular skirt and, in turn, the satin benefits by the flare treatment. What better reason is needed for their combination in this model?

The treatment of the waist is one that harmonizes very well with the rippled skirt, for the sides, not being shaped and held together in a under-arm seam, fall in soft folds over the arm and, in addition, a long scarf effect ripples down the back from one shoulder.

Wallflower, which may be described as a soft, dark henna, is the color of the satin, with waist-line ornaments of tangerine and green contributing the only contrast.

As a rule, 5½ yards of 40-inch material is sufficient for a design such as this.

In making the dress, face the under-arm portions with the material, applying these facings over the waist lining. Cut the drapery in one with the surplice front, first modeling this in muslin so as to insure correct results.

Model 4D.—Over a camisole and plain-skirt foundation of satin, the loose, crêpe-chiffon blouse and circular draperies of this design ripple in a most enchanting manner with every movement of the figure. Both the satin and the chiffon are of black, but crystal beading on the blouse and picoted ribbons of bright blue, black, and metallic silver at the waist line provide notes that serve to emphasize the suitability of the design for a slender or youthful type. The style is one that suggests evening or dinner wear, but it is suitable, also, for formal afternoon affairs.

Provide about 2½ yards of satin and 5 yards of chiffon for the average figure, with 1 yard of ribbon of each color.

In modeling the skirt draperies, use circular pieces cut about 27 inches wide at the upper edge and 12 inches wide at the bottom. You might outline pieces of this shape on a gathered circular-skirt pattern.

Variety in Sleeves.—Fashion is showing so much variation in sleeve designs this season, that regardless of how many frocks are included in one's wardrobe a different sleeve treatment for each should be the rule.

Very often sleeves show kimono influence, whether they are cut in one with the front of the waist or, as at *a*, set into a very deep armhole. This design has a trimming strip of self-material running the entire length of its center and cut in one with the band that finishes the lower edge. Novelty braid in Persian colorings, a trimming of prominence this season, might be substituted for the band of self-material. The arrangement of self-covered buttons is interesting. With a trimming piece of self-material, however, the buttons might be of the filigree variety.

Over a sleeve that is flared to a point below the elbow and then tapered to a close-fitting wrist line, a cuff or trimming band applied in saw-tooth effect gives a semblance of a double cuff, as at *b*.

A pretty, youthful arm most assuredly justifies the use of a sleeve like the one shown at *c*. This consists merely of a straight plaited strip of material joined at a dropped armhole and confined at the wrist line with a rosette-finished ribbon.

The more conservative type of sleeve shown at *d* may be chosen by the mature woman. Suggestive of dignity in its cut and simple decoration of embroidery, it would add considerable distinction to a costume, provided a matching bit of embroidery were carried out on some other part of the dress.

Draped Dress

Fresh impetus to the vogue for draped models is the assurance carried by the newest fabrics, for a suppleness that surpasses any previous offerings in materials seems to be the general characteristic. And draperies are appearing on every side in such variety of interpretations that there is no difficulty in finding a drape to suit every purpose and every type. Besides, it is an easy matter to select a drapery that is strictly within the limit of one's ability to achieve, for draperies range from straight applied strips, which even the beginner in dressmaking would have no difficulty in applying, to the most intricate handling of the material, which requires the skill of an artist.

The preeminence of the side-draped model makes this the noteworthy feature for fall styles, but there seems to be a well-established rumor of the approach of center-front draperies, which will concentrate most of the skirt fulness at the front and cause the back skirt portion, in marked contrast, to be drawn closely over the figure and clearly define its lines. Even in many prevalent styles, the back skirt portion has a tantalizing habit of differing so decidedly from the front that one cannot immediately relate the two.

Among the loveliest and most practical of the side-draped models, the design shown here may surely take its stand. This is fashioned of black crêpe-back satin, a material that lends itself admirably to draping. The front is in one piece with unbroken effect at the waist line, but the back has a separate gathered skirt portion. White broadcloth decorated with cut-work and edged with bright green grosgrain ribbon forms the collar and also provides sleeves trimming bands. The grosgrain ribbon appears again in the rosette that holds the drapery.

Material and Pattern Requirements.—For the average figure, 5 yards of 40-inch material, ⅜ yard for the collar and sleeve bands, and 3 yards of ribbon are needed.

If you are unable to procure a pattern having a one-piece draped front similar to this, you may use a plain one-piece front for cutting the muslin model, leaving an allowance for the extension at the left side. Then, in developing the model, lift the material at the side to form the drapery and pin this in position, afterwards shaping the lower edge as you desire it.

For the back skirt portion, you may provide merely a staight length of material wide enough to extend under the drapery at the left side.

Construction and Fitting.—Gather the back skirt portion and baste this flat to the waist, leaving an extension at the left side, as provided in the cutting, for the part that extends under the drapery. Then baste the seams, but, before stitching, slip on the dress and observe all the points that should be noted in the first fitting.

After the fitting, finish the seams; then make the collar and the sleeve trimming bands ready for application. If you are using broadcloth of firm weave and wish to decorate this with cut-work, instead of securing the raw edges with embroidery floss in the usual manner, you may merely outline the designs with very fine machine stitching in self-color and afterwards cut close to the stitching Finish the outer edge of the collar and sleeve bands with bindings of ribbon and then baste them in position.

For the back girdle portion, cut a bias strip about 7 inches wide and several inches longer than one-half the measurement taken at a low waist line. For a dress of this kind, the waist line is generally made but a few inches above the normal hip line. Finish the edges of the girdle by turning them under and securing them flat with extremely fine stitches.

In the second fitting, pin the drapery in position and then pin this to the waist-line fulness of the extension made on the back skirt portion. Arrange the girdle so that it may be tacked at the right under arm and finished with the left under arm to extend just under the drapery and be secured each time the dress is put on. This adjustment will make it possible to slip the dress over the head with ease even though there is no other than the neck opening.

If you desire a soft finish across the front neck line, pin a double fold of self-colored chiffon or Georgette in position, as shown. Then turn an even line at the lower edge, pin the edge of the back skirt extension just inside of the drapery, and observe whether the drapery is correct.

Finishing.—Finish the lower edge of the skirt and drapery with wide bias bindings and tack the underneath skirt portion to the lower edge of the one-piece front.

Finish the ends of the girdle for proper adjustment and place facings over all the joinings where overcasted edges would not prove satisfactory.

Make the rosette of separate pieces of ribbon cut with pointed ends, arranging them in pinwheel fashion; then tack this over the drapery at the side front.

Unique Development of Double Brims

Simple and of utmost chic is this huge black Lyons velvet hat, a canotier of cartwheel propensities, which is flanged midway on the under brim with a hanging veil effect of Chantilly lace.

A rather high oval crown with straight brim about 3 inches wide is used for the foundation, the under brim being covered plain with silver cloth. A row of Chantilly lace, 2 inches wide, is sewed on the top of the brim around the edge and allowed to hang in a veil effect over the eyes.

The upper brim, which extends about 3 inches beyond this edge, is made of two layers of velvet and one of crinoline pasted together. Usually, no wire is needed on the edge of this type brim, because the pasting of the velvet to the crinoline gives enough stiffness, but in some cases a lace wire may be used, after which the edge can be bound with a row of grosgrain ribbon or a narrow bias binding of the velvet.

A balloon crown of velvet is drawn down over the foundation and draped in soft folds around the side crown, and a spray of metal and velvet flowers adorns its right side front.

Model 5

Vintage Notions Monthly ©2016 Amy Barickman, LLC

Look for a collectible print version at the end of this issue.

Variations of Draped Dress

Model 5A.—Subtleness lurks in the drapery of this navy crêpe satin model, for each turn of the figure brings a new conception of the manner in which the skirt is developed. The most pronounced portion of the drapery is at the right side where the material is drawn up toward the side back and laid in plaits, thus causing the cascade folds. This drapery is cut in one with the front portion of the skirt, which is extended to the left side back and joined, with a narrow drapery of the applied variety, to the back skirt section. The back skirt section, in turn, is extended under the right side drapery and tacked to this.

Over the kimono foundation of the waist are laid front and back panels, which broaden toward the waist line until they meet at the under arm. The front panel boasts particular novelty in the manner in which it extends over the shoulders and terminates in loose-hanging straps finished at the ends with deep fringe that matches the dress in color. The cuffs are of the panel variety, having the ends finished separately.

For the average figure, 5¼ yards of 40-inch material are needed for the development of this model.

Model 5B.—There seems to be no other color that can combine its decidedly contrasting tones to produce nearly so much charm as the gradations of brown. Perhaps this is the reason why brown and tan combinations have lasted through a number of seasons and still prove of irresistible appeal in models such as this draped velvet dress, which is of a dark brown termed Hindu, with drapery and sleeve facings and a trimming piece accenting the side closing of the waist, of toast-colored crêpe satin.

The drapery is cut in one with the skirt, one end of the material being dropped at the side to form the cascade effect and the opposite end secured under this drapery. The rosette is of velvet faced with the contrasting fabric.

Average material requirements for this design are 4½ yards of velvet and 1¼ yards of crêpe satin.

Model 5C.—Fulness "pinched in" and also secured with shirrings at each side waist line in the unbelted one-piece front stamps this model as of the newer mode. The material is crêpe satin and the color, Rangoon, a brown several tones lighter than Hindu. The back is cut in two-piece fashion, having a waist panel that repeats the front effect and narrow skirt panels at each side back. These panels are lined with chiffon and this same material is used for facing the lower edge of the broad kimono sleeves. The ornaments over the draperies are of bronze beads.

Provide, for the average figure, about 5 yards of crêpe satin and 1¼ yards of chiffon.

Model 5D.—To soar in the very heights of draped distinction, a model has but to choose velvet as its fabric and then draw up its fulness at one side in soft, lovely folds. Such requirements have been met most delightfully in this evening gown of coral-colored chiffon velvet, and, in addition, grape designs formed of crystal beads for the grape clusters and silver cloth appliqué for the leaves, provide a trimming that is in exquisite contrast with the velvety coral background.

This same trimming might also be used with excellent effect on white velvet and, really, a safer selection than white velvet for fall and winter wear would be difficult to make, for white is assured great popularity for the coming season. The design is one that has possibilities, also, as an afternoon costume, for it might be developed from Canton crêpe of a becoming color and the grape designs made of small oval-shaped sections of material picoted around the edge and tacked merely at the upper end in cluster arrangement, and the leaves made of picoted sections of metal cloth.

About 4 yards of velvet is needed to develop the model as illustrated, which does not make allowance for the foundation skirt included in the pattern suggested for this design. For trimming, provide ½ yard of silver cloth and 3 small bunches of beads.

Model 5E.—An inevitable part of the smart wardrobe is a black dress so fashioned that it may serve as either a dinner or an evening gown and thus solve the problem of what to wear when one is in doubt as to the nature of some function one contemplates attending.

Just such a dress is this model of crêpe chiffon, which combines two kinds of drapery, the "pinched-in" variety at each side to indicate the waist line, and the applied cascade type, lace being used to carry out this effect. The front portion of the waist is cut to carry out a cascade drapery similar to that formed by the lace in the back and is picoted on its edges and tacked in one or two places to the lace on the shoulder. A jet girdle extends across the back waist line and terminates at each side front in very attractive jet ornaments. The foundation slip, cut in camisole fashion at the top, is of soft satin.

For the average figure, provide 3 yards of chiffon, 2¾ yards of lace, and 2¾ yards of satin.

Model 5F.—Annoyances and difficulties that ever seem to be synonymous with the fitting and adjusting of sleeves of the regulation type fade into the background when sleeves of the type shown here make their appearance. These consist merely of a broad strip of material shaped a trifle at the upper edge and applied by merely laying it over the waist portion and securing the slightly shaped edge, leaving all the other edges free.

Toast-colored Panama crêpe, a fabric similar in appearance to Canton crêpe but with its under surface more downy and showing a less decided rib, is used for this model. A cascade drapery cut in one with the front of the skirt and an accordion-plaited strip of the material merely looped over the belt distinguish the otherwise plain skirt. The belt and sleeve trimming is of red beads.

About 5 yards of material 40 inches wide is needed to make this model for the average figure.

Economy Dresses

When economy must, of necessity, be the uppermost thought in the selection of a dress, this need not mean that style must be sacrificed, for careful planning of a costume may result in a happy combination of both of these qualities. First of all, there are colors and materials to consider. Standard colors, black, navy, and brown, are always safe selections, for their unobtrusiveness makes for less concern when the dress must be worn again and again in the same company. Materials must be of the less expensive varieties, but never cheap in appearance.

In the matter of design, the point to consider is whether the economy dress must serve for several seasons or whether, because of its inexpensiveness, it may be planned with only one or two seasons' wear in view. In the one case, conservativeness of style must be dominant; in the other, a bit of the extreme may be indulged in.

Right in line with talk of economy dresses is the virtue of careful remodeling. Oftentimes, a frock that bears style marks of several seasons past, by careful renovating and a little recutting or the addition of some new touches, may be made to take the place of an entirely new model.

Model 6.—That drawn-thread work need not depend entirely on summer fabrics for effectiveness is the opinion gained from this simple one-piece model of an inexpensive quality of navy wool crêpe. Besides, the drawing and hemstitching of coarse woolen threads cannot be termed at all tedious in comparison with the work required on frail cotton fibers.

Outside of the drawn-thread work, the making of this model is extremely simple, for there are merely the under-arm seams, the hem, the belt, and the neck and sleeve bindings, which are of red silk, to consider.

Provided one's piece bag may be resorted to for bindings, the only purchase for this dress need be 3½ yards of material 44 to 54 inches wide.

Model 6A.—When a dress is kept to a comparatively small yardage and no extra allowance made for trimmings one naturally expects it to be very conservative and perhaps a bit uninteresting as to character. But two such handicaps are most gracefully overcome in this model of black silk crêpe, which is frankly a style of up-to-the-minute smartness.

The skirt is of two straight pieces, the front portion having its sides left free for a distance of 8 or 10 inches at the upper edge, which permits them to fall in cascade effect. Between the draperies at the upper edge are four or five narrow tucks pressed in upstanding fashion, and these, with similar tucks placed in the lower portion of the straight-line bodice, form a wide girdle effect. Narrow sash ends brought from the under-arm seams and tied at the center back cover the joining of the plain gathered back skirt portion to the tucked bodice. The sides of this back skirt portion are slip-stitched under the draperies formed by the front.

Double, unpressed bias strips of self-material arranged in parallel rows and circular motifs provide the novel yoke and sleeve trimming bands.

For the average figure, provide 4¼ yards of material.

Model 6B.—A means of modernizing a past season's dress is suggested by this design, which, as illustrated, is of navy serge with red jersey front panel and cuffs decorated with groups of large navy French knots.

One of the most notably out-of-date features of a dress may be its comparatively high waist line. A seam above the waist line, arranged as in this model, makes the piecing a success, provided discarded portions of the dress are sufficiently large to permit the cutting of these piecings. The skirt joined at a low waist line and faced rather than hemmed will surely prove long enough, and the insertions of contrasting material will provide extra width if this is needed. In the sleeves, the contrasting fabric may take the place of a worn portion.

To develop the entire design for the average figure, 3½ yards of material 44 inches wide, 1⅛ yards for trimming, and 1 skein of floss are needed.

Model 6C.—Crêpe de Chine, crêpella, which is a wool crêpe, or serge, all of which are inexpensive fabrics, might be used for this very simple, even though entirely smart, model. As shown, it is of black crêpe de Chine, with narrow vestee and sleeve facings of the same material in jade green, a waist-line ornament of jade, and narrow black ribbon ends that extend from under the collar.

Without a generous use of material, the skirt contrives to achieve distinction through its long panel on the right and its front portion, which is lifted in a mere suggestion of a drape at the left side and extended around to the side back.

About 4½ yards of 40-inch material and ½ yard for trimming are needed to develop a model such as this for the average figure.

Accentuating Right-Side Trim

While simply-made hats are desired for general wear, great latitude is allowed in the trimming, burnt peacock, coque, and ostrich, both natural and metallized, being favored, as shown in these models.

Duvetyn and panne velvet are employed in the construction of the hat shown in Model 6. For the brim, a bias strip of duvetyn ⅝ yard wide and 40 inches long is joined in a ring, and three rows of shirring ⅜ inch apart are run around each edge. This strip is then laid over a 2½-inch-wide foundation frame and the shirring drawn up to fit the head-size on top and underneath.

The four-piece sectional crown is developed according to the method given for making a six-piece crown in Art. 37, *Piece Goods Hats*. In developing the four-piece sectional, it will be necessary to allow an extra 2 inches across the bottom of each section, making it 6 inches, and to graduate the sides in the right proportion. These sections are outlined with a cord of duvetyn before being joined and then applied to the brim.

Model 6

6A

6B

6C

Vintage Notions Monthly ©2016 Amy Barickman, LLC

Magic Pattern: One Sleeved Bias Scarf

> This is an original Magic Pattern, a project you cut out using diagrams instead of pattern pieces. These were first created by Mary Brooks Picken for the Woman's Institute's student magazines, *Inspiration* and *Fashion Service*. My book **Vintage Notions: An Inspirational Guide to Needlework, Cooking, Sewing, Fashion & Fun** featured 12 original Magic Patterns. Recently I have created modern patterns that were inspired by these vintage gems featured in the book **The Magic Pattern Book**, which I licensed with Workman Publishing. We have chosen to keep the authenticity of this original pattern intact and therefore have not changed instructions based on modern fabrics and techniques. Note at the end of this pattern you will find helpful tips for drafting pattern pieces.

▶▶▶ THIS IS a new twist on an old idea. Have you despaired of keeping a scarf on your shoulders and attractively draped? The sleeve effect in this scarf is your answer.

You need 1 yd. to 1⅛ yd. of 50-in. taffeta. Follow the same diagram for cutting a yard of fabric, but make the diagonal ends shorter.

To cut out: Straighten fabric. Lay it flat, with one raw edge toward you. Point A is at upper left-hand corner. B is 10 in. to left of lower right-hand corner. Chalk a line diagonally from A to B. Using this line as a guide, measure and outline scarf pieces as indicated on diagram. Cut out on heavy outlines.

To make: Bring edges C and D together so that front and back are lapped, as in E. Seam edges at F to make shoulder line and edges at G to form underarm. Turn seams to inside and press. Finish all edges with narrow rolled hems.

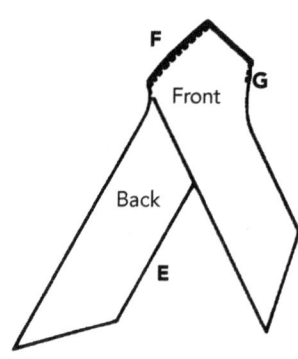

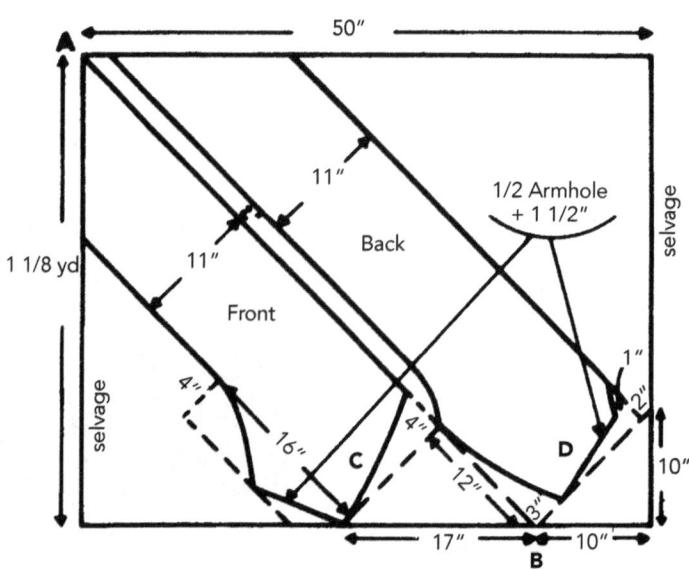

Your Measurement Chart & Notes on Making Magic Patterns

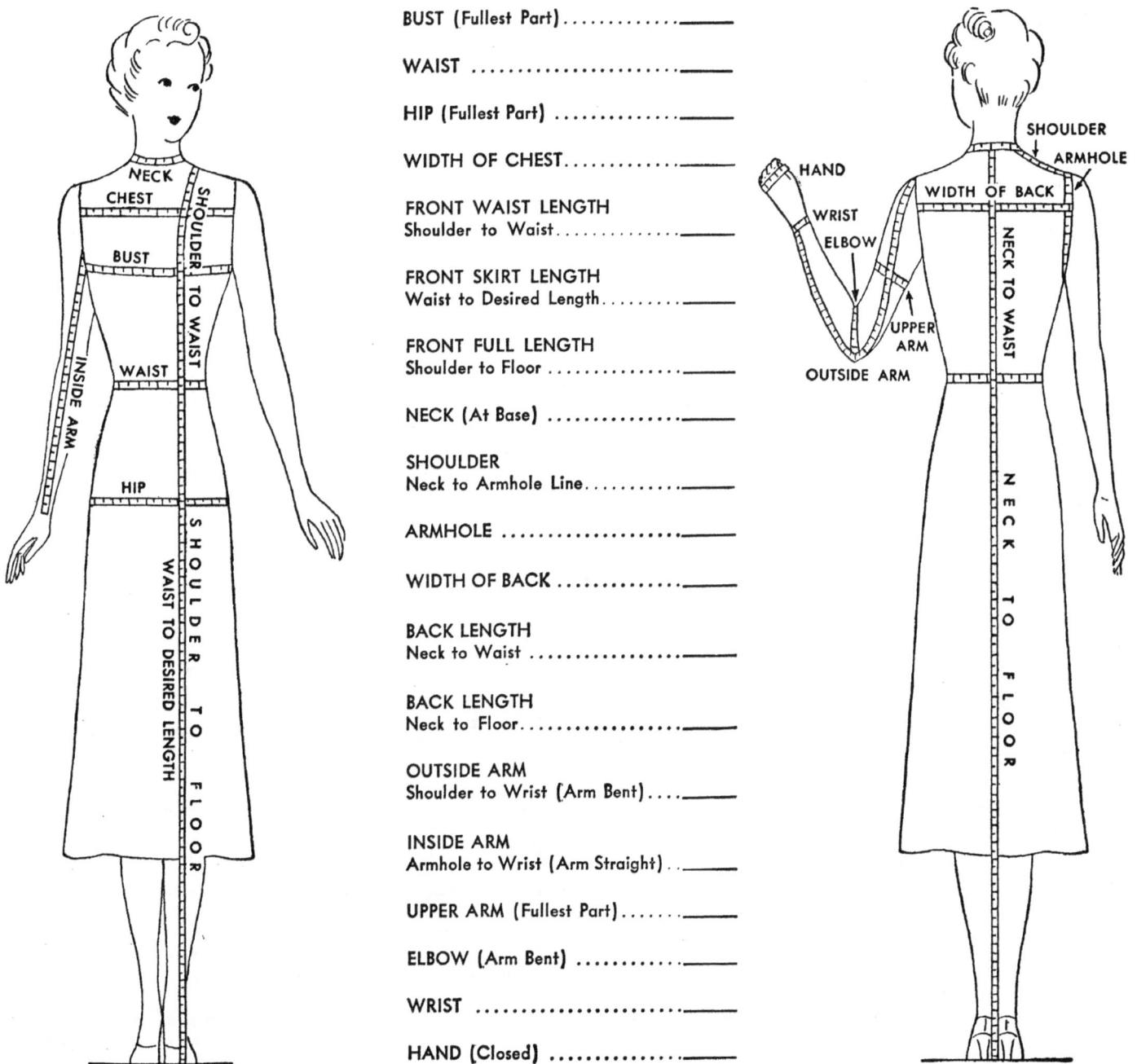

BUST (Fullest Part) ...._____

WAIST ...._____

HIP (Fullest Part) ...._____

WIDTH OF CHEST............_____

FRONT WAIST LENGTH
Shoulder to Waist............_____

FRONT SKIRT LENGTH
Waist to Desired Length........_____

FRONT FULL LENGTH
Shoulder to Floor ...._____

NECK (At Base) ...._____

SHOULDER
Neck to Armhole Line............_____

ARMHOLE ...._____

WIDTH OF BACK ...._____

BACK LENGTH
Neck to Waist ...._____

BACK LENGTH
Neck to Floor..................._____

OUTSIDE ARM
Shoulder to Wrist (Arm Bent)...._____

INSIDE ARM
Armhole to Wrist (Arm Straight).._____

UPPER ARM (Fullest Part)......._____

ELBOW (Arm Bent) ...._____

WRIST ...._____

HAND (Closed) ...._____

Keep Accurate Measurements

Since the garments in this book are all cut from measurements, it is necessary to have accurate ones to follow. Keep a list of your own measurements always at hand for ready reference.

Measurements for fitted garments should be taken over the type of foundation garments you expect to wear with them. Remove dress, jacket, or coat, which would distort the measurements. Do not take measurements too tight. Make all easy enough for comfort. The chart shows how to place the tape correctly for each measurement.

Making The Pattern

If you have the least doubt about your ability to chalk out the garment on your fabric, then rough it out first with crayon or heavy pencil on wrapping paper or newspaper. Cut out the paper pattern and use it to cut your garment. Cutting from a diagram, you can be sure that the proportions are correct for your size and that the garment will be a good fit.

Becomingness, a Hat's Chief Asset

By MARY MAHON
Department of Millinery

REGARDLESS of the fabric or trimming chosen for a hat, it must possess the element of youth and must be becoming to the wearer if it is to be a success and top the costume properly. And it is gratifying to see how amazingly youthful the newest hats are. Their colorings are bright, their contour is close, and many of them dazzle with metallic trimmings. With so much of charm and beauty from which to select, it is almost impossible to err in one's choice if the idea of becomingness is kept in mind.

A feature of utmost importance in the season's modes is the fact that, with the present styles, the art of millinery is gradually returning. Expert workmanship, cleverness in hand-blocking, and general manipulation of the lines of the hat must be heeded carefully since careless making cannot be covered up by additional trimming. Even trimming, though extremely simple, is carefully thought out, and requires the deft fingers of the clever milliner to apply it. Whether the fabric should repeat that of the rest of the attire or be metallic, velvet, or felt is a question that each individual must decide for herself.

GROUPED on this page for illustration are various types of mid-winter hats, all of which demonstrate the very popular idea of securing smart effects with self-material trims or novel ornaments. Stylists, in search of something new, have gone far afield for some, such as the baby calf now so much the vogue, and have found new ways of treatment for old favorites, such as pony skin. Both of these furs are so treated that they are as flexible as cloth, and milliners are using them in much the same way, taking unprecedented liberties with distinct success.

The hat at the extreme left, a close-back, drooping-front-brim toque, has its top brim fitted plain with baby calf, and its soft crown, which follows the backward draped movement of the early fall, fashioned out of heavy black satin. As if to hold the folds in position on the center front of the crown, a long slender triangle of the calf is appliquéd in a slightly slanting line and serves as the decorative trim for this model.

THE best hats are still soft and supple and in no way severe. Their restrained quality comes, not from poverty of ideas, but from great knowledge, great technical perfection, and a true conception of sophisticated simplicity, as portrayed in the model at the left of the center. This medium-wide brim of supple felt is topped with a generous tam crown of the same material. Several bands of narrow metallic ribbon are run through slashes so as to form a basket-weave effect about 2 inches wide at the base of the crown. For the trim, an ostrich flower is applied in a dent at the left front of the crown.

This type of crown affords many possibilities in the way of manipulation. It can be creased and dented to suit the short woman, being shaped to give decided height at the direct back, side, or at any point to make the hat becoming. For the tall woman, it may assume the broad, flat effect here shown.

THE model at the right of the center features the broad, tam-crown effect, except that in this instance it accompanies a narrow drooping brim. In this petite hat, very definite lines are conspicious by their absence, that is, a soft yielding effect is stressed. Becomingness is the cue taken up by the designer. The size of the brim is a studied perfection, being cut and drooped a trifle and then bound with a narrow binding of calf skin. Inserted in the crown at each side of the front are two motifs of the same calf skin, introduced to give color and interest. An amber hairpin, set in brilliants, is thrust through a crease in the crown at the right side, giving the hat a smart note.

SUGGESTIVE of spring is the hat illustrated at the extreme right. Black satin, bright metallic brocade, and gay feather flowers set low at the right side of the crown blend their way into this smart hat. This model, too, boasts of a narrow, eye-shading brim, which is covered plain with the satin and bound with a narrow metallic ribbon. The medium-high, dented crown is covered with metallic cloth. A V-shaped motif of satin starts at the base of the crown in the center front and spreads out over the dented top. Attached low at the right-side back and extending beyond the brim edge are several feather flowers, giving a softening effect to an otherwise stiff hat.

For formal wear, the vogue for metallic brocade effects lends its charm to the simple wrap shown at the lower center. A 40-inch-wide square of brocade has its four sides edged with a 9-inch-wide double binding of satin.

THE hat modes of the hour are replete with youthful and becoming styles, which will inevitably work their way into the early spring modes. This is particularly true of the present vogue for metallic and tinsel, which are carried over for the southern resort wear and the early spring season, not in the splashy effects used for winter but in discreet touches, as shown in the new mouchon body hat, which has the single sequins worked in with the weave at wide intervals. This body and the metallic transparent hats and the Georgette-covered felts are the forerunners of the new season.

Comfort, pliability, and youthfulness are the requisites of the new hats for resort and spring wear. No matter whether straw or fabric is employed in their construction, the finished hat must have the same soft silhouette and smartness that have made the felt an item all women are loathe to relinquish.

SPECIAL emphasis is placed on color this season. With very few exceptions, every one can wear black, for it means absence of color, and the pale woman, as well as the one with high color, looks quite well in it. Because of its serviceable and easy-to-wear properties, women have drifted into the wearing of black and dark neutral shades and have become habituated to them, the result being that many of them appear dull and inanimate. But these very women, dressed in bright colors, are rejuvenated and, in living up to such colors, often show very different personalities. For this reason, stylists are stressing color, and in working with the individual, are endeavoring not only to supply a contrasting note to her ensemble but to bring out her best features by the color used in her hat.

Originally published in Inspiration, *1927.*

Artful *Simplicity* in *Hair* Dress

By BARBARA ELLISON
Department of Good Looks

AS one looks out over a gathering of women, it is interesting to observe the types of hair dress and to speculate how this or that effect is achieved. Simplicity is the dominant theme, but it is an artful simplicity. Let no woman think that she may avoid taking trouble by bobbing her hair, for by doing so she draws the line between becomingness and unbecomingness much more sharply, and consequently dare not permit the least slipping into carelessness. Ends that have grown a bit scraggly or that stand out when they should be turned under, oiliness instead of glossiness, or a harsh, starchy look when there should be softness and luster, are fatal to the effect she wishes to secure. And so, more than ever, the price that she pays for beauty must be eternal vigilance.

The carefully groomed woman possesses a genius for detail. She understands that before she touches the comb to her hair to arrange it, she must give it the care that it needs to look its best.

THE first question most women ask is, "How often should I shampoo my hair to keep it in good condition?" You must depend a good deal on your own judgment for this, taking into consideration the nature of your hair and the surroundings in which you live and work. But often enough, certainly, to keep the hair and scalp clean, for cleanliness is one of the first requirements of hair health and beauty. Short hair should be washed oftener than long because it does not protect the scalp so well from dust and soil and also because the oil that would naturally have more surface over which to distribute itself is confined to shorter lengths and is consequently more profuse.

Before washing the hair, brush it well. Then wet hair and scalp thoroughly with warm water, and with the tips of the fingers rub whatever cleaning agent you use well into the scalp and through the ends of the hair until you have worked up a good lather. Rinse in warm water and lather again; then rinse in at least three waters until the water runs clear, using lemon juice in the next to the last rinse if you require a special agent to remove all traces of soap. The first lathering cleans the hair while the second brings out its lights and glints.

THE blood being the only carrier of nourishment to the hair, a scalp through which the blood circulates sluggishly is an undernourished scalp and generally produces thin, lusterless hair. And the reverse is true, that a scalp in which the blood courses actively almost invariably grows shining, healthy hair. So you will understand the virtue of massage in keeping up the appearance of the hair.

About ten minutes each night should be given to the stimulation of the scalp. Separate the hair, placing the tips of the fingers on the scalp with a firm, but not heavy, pressure, and move the fingers in a circular motion without lifting them. Work back from the top or sides of the head to the neck until the whole scalp has been gone over, finishing with a fairly vigorous rubbing of the shoulders and back of the neck to drive the circulation upward to the scalp. Such massage will not tire you if you place your elbows on a table and bend forward with your head between your hands.

If your scalp is exceptionally dry, rub in a little oil of sweet almonds before you begin to massage it. A good way to apply the oil is with a medicine dropper. Be careful to get it directly on the scalp and not on the hair.

Another way to stimulate the circulation, and an excellent one, is to pull the hair. Pick it up strand by strand, and, holding it firmly close to the scalp, give a strong, but not a jerky, pull. This treatment is good for both dry and oily hair, going far toward restoring the health and tone of any scalp and thereby correcting conditions either of excessive oiliness or dryness.

IN arranging long hair according to the present mode, the contour of the head must be revealed, too much hair easily detracting from smartness. In the illustration at the upper left is an arrangement that suggests a gracefully becoming bob, the soft knot at the back being fashionably inconspicuous.

To secure a fashionable effect, keep the hair short and thinned out. Or, if you object to cutting it, try arranging it somewhat after the following manner:

Separate the front and bring it forward to be arranged later. Divide the remaining portion, leaving a thin fringe at the back, coil the rest over the back of the head in as flat an effect as possible, and pin secure. Then bring the front over the back, and, together with the fringe at the neck, form it into a small knot or other inconspicuous arrangement to produce an effect similar to that shown.

THE mannish bob, which was becoming to only a few, is fast passing from the mode. So says Monsieur Manuel, the famous dictator of hair fashions. And we should, perhaps, be glad that its vogue is over, for it was a peculiarly trying type of hair dress.

The bob of the hour clings to the head, but it is soft and graceful in effect, as shown at the right above. Here, too, a quantity of hair is undesirable and should be carefully thinned out underneath by a competent hair-dresser if it threatens to produce undesirable bulk at any spot, for always the well-shaped contour of the head should stand revealed. The Bobbie Pin, by the way, which is like a narrow steel spring, is very helpful in holding wayward locks close to the head.

The more you see and study the sleek hair dresses of the present day, the more you come to appreciate the natural beauty of a well-shaped head and the more you desire to see it untampered with. It becomes actually distressing sometimes, therefore, to look at a head shortened in the back by a hair cut that begins an inch or more above the natural line and is perhaps further chopped off by being cut straight across. In contrast to this, observe, if you will, the manner in which the natural hair line is followed in the illustration.

WHILE hair very beautifully waved is always attractive, one becomes almost satiated at times with the regularity and sameness of the marcel and occasionally looks with distinct pleasure at perfectly straight hair on just the right type of woman. Such a mode is by no means easy to wear, but when it is becoming, it possesses the advantage of being distinctive and of lending itself to effects that are what the Parisians call "chic."

When the hair is waved, the almost universal preference is for the deep, soft, natural-looking wave. If your hair is such that it responds to a water wave, choose this, for it eliminates the devastating heat of the iron.

There is also on the market a new preparation that is intended to give almost instantaneous results, also without the application of heat. The hair is first wet and combed with a waving fluid, after which a natural-looking wave may be set with the fingers. The hair is then allowed to dry, when the waves may be combed out without losing their permanency.

It is claimed that this fluid is neither sticky nor greasy and that it will hold a wave for a week at least.

The Modern Woman

By ALICE M. STONE
Editorial Department

WE hear much these days about the faults of the modern woman and her lack of interest in housewifely arts, but such a picture, as applied to the average woman, leaves us unconvinced when we constantly receive such letters as these.

"It seems as though every time I pick up a needle or open the machine," writes Mrs. Mildred E. Murphy, a California student, "I have more to thank you for. My little three-year-old girl is the neatest dressed babe in our block and I've made every stitch she wears. We are making a trip East soon, and every bit of Madeline's and my wardrobe, I have made. She has ten dresses and three of them have hats to match, while I have just one dozen. My coat is four years old, but you'd never know it.

"My husband says I'm worth a mint for what I save. My outfit and the babe's, enough to last us until next season, have cost under $50.00."

Ends Complaint, "I Have Nothing to Wear"

"AT the time of my marriage," says Mrs. Irma I. Imhof, an Ohio member, "the subject of clothes did not trouble me much because I had money to buy the pretty clothes I am so fond of. But later I realized what a problem it is to make a dollar go far when you are paying for a home and furniture.

"My husband was just as generous as any husband ever was, but the ready-made garments that I liked to wear seemed so expensive, and each time I needed a new garment the situation became more serious to me.

"Finally I wrote to the Woman's Institute for literature, and decided I would purchase the course if my husband would consent. At first he doubted whether any one could learn to sew by mail, but he finally consented, and I enrolled.

"After the first few lessons I began making plain things, and soon after I was making pretty dresses. I have just completed two beautiful Georgette gowns. One of them cost me $8.50 and the other $11.00, and had I been forced to purchase them at the store, I would have had to pay at least $40.00 for each. I know because I saw some that were no prettier for that price.

"My husband says the best part of it is I never complain that I have nothing fit to wear now, and he is as happy about what I have accomplished as I am.

"I have saved many times the cost of the course on my own clothes, besides the money I have earned sewing for others."

How to Stretch the Clothes Budget

"FOR the last fourteen months," says Mrs. Edwin Jeffrey, a Canadian student, "I have not bought a single ready-made garment for myself or my four children, and they are a lot better dressed than they have ever been. I have more dresses, too, than I have had since I was married.

"I had a doctor's bill of $149.00 last winter when my husband was very sick with pneumonia, and it is paid chiefly because I made our clothes this year. We have had more picnics and outings this summer, too, than during the last three summers put together."

Her Training Envied by All Her Friends

NATURAL regret over lost opportunities, as glimpsed in the following letter from Miss Helen H. Zeintck, a New York State girl, makes one realize keenly the virtue of securing one's training before the chance has slipped by and the need for it has become an acute stimulus. Miss Zeintck's own experience, by way of contrast, is doubly satisfying.

"My mother has been a widow for over twenty-one years," she writes. "When Father died, there were three of us left and very little cash. I went to a nearby factory, and as soon as I could take care of a machine, received $7.00 a week.

"One day I bought a magazine, and looking it over noticed the advertisement of the Institute. Outside of a few middy blouses and things made during my last school year, I didn't have anything to wear, so I sent for particulars and enrolled.

"When the first books came, I was overcome with joy to think that anything could be so simple, and it remained that way right through the course.

"A few years ago I thought it would be nice for some of my friends to enroll, but they told me that they could not be bothered. Quite recently these girls came back. They are married now, and they insist that I instruct them at home. But it's too late. I enter a training school this fall, so it's quite out of the question.

"My clothes spell not only individuality and personality but that little something that is so different, and are envied by all my friends. And when you take into consideration the wonderful saving (in four years I have saved $500), why I assure you that, regardless of difficulties, cost, or any other obstacle, I would take the course again."

The Money-Makers

Could *YOU* Use More Money?

Yes—yes—yes—came the chorus. From Mrs. Brown, whose little Mary had outgrown all of last year's clothes and needed new from head to toe—Mrs. Grey, with two big boys in college, who try to be considerate of Dad, but who just had to have some of the necessities—Betty White, with an income, but too small to provide the fur coat that the furrier said he would hold for her until her deposit was ready—Sylvia Green, the teacher, who last summer had her first taste of travel and this year expects to see something of Europe. A very emphatic *Yes* from Gertrude Brown, newlywed. She can't get used to asking her Tom for spending money, so wants to earn her own.

"How can we earn some extra dollars, just in our spare time?" is what these ambitious folks wrote us. And here is the answer. The Christmas Money Club, which started in September, provided extra dollars—all their own—for so many of our Woman's Institute friends that we are going to continue the club plan. These folks who have been earning both Commission and Bonus have proved themselves real "Money-Makers," so this new plan for earning extra dollars in just one's spare moments is to be named after them—"The Money-Makers."

How You Can Be a Money-Maker

You will want to know all about this pleasant, easy way to earn some extra money for many of the little things that mean so much to one's happiness, but of which only too often one is deprived.

There is nothing hard about it. It is merely the difference between *losing* spare moments and *putting them to work for you.*

In just their spare moments, other women are now earning extra dollars that provide the things they have longed for, and the Institute will help *you*, too, to earn a fund all your own to do with as you like.

Read the Circular sent with this copy of INSPIRATION, fill in the coupon, or, if the Circular has been mislaid, just send us a card asking how you, too, can become a Money-Maker. We want to help you so—

Resolve Today to Be a 1927 Money-Maker

Cross-Stitch and Needle-Point

By CLARICE CARPENTER
Editorial Department

THE quaint charm of cross-stitch is unsurpassed by any other type of needlework, for about it there lingers the romance of its association with the old-time samplers, which had their origin in Europe long before America was discovered. Recently there has been a revival of interest in the sampler, and one now sees many prized examples that have come down from our own colonial days, as well as very modern ones characterized by a lightness of sentiment that links them with the spirit of modern interior decoration both in color and in motif.

Of the latter type, the one illustrated at the right is a splendid example. The little maid, who so heartily asserts her willingness to attempt musical impossibilities, stands out very charmingly in black cross-stitch on white linen. Edging the sampler is a floral border in pink, blue, and green. It is framed in a simple, narrow, black frame.

But cross-stitch is by no means confined to samplers. In simple motifs and borders, it makes the most delightful decoration imaginable for children's clothes, underwear, blouses, handkerchiefs, and innumerable household linens. By varying the colors, the size of the stitches, and the kind and size of thread, a great number of effects may be obtained from a single pattern.

THERE are so many ways of making cross-stitch that one should first learn something of each method and then choose the one best adapted to one's needs. Perhaps the simplest way is to follow a pattern stamped on the material, although this method has certain drawbacks. It is almost impossible to transfer the pattern so accurately that it follows threads of the material exactly and the blue lines of the transfer may show through the stitches after the work is completed. But for lingerie and children's dresses that are to be laundered, it is very satisfactory, and does indeed save time.

The original method is probably the one of counting the threads of the fabric and working over the same number of threads in both directions for each stitch. And undoubtedly it is the most accurate one. For this, the warp and woof threads must be the same size, and unless they are fairly coarse, the work is hard on the eyes. An exception, however, is found in such fabrics as cross-barred dimity and finely checked ginghams.

The most used method is that of working the design over cross-stitch canvas basted to the material, afterwards removing the canvas by pulling it out, thread by thread, thus leaving the cross-stitching on the fabric underneath. Designs to be used in this way are of two kinds, printed on cross-barred paper. One has the design printed in colors, each square in the color intended for the cross-stitch that it represents. The other is a black-and-white diagram with each square marked by a color symbol. A chart explaining the color represented by each symbol accompanies such a diagram. Designs for filet crochet may also be used, the worker carrying out her own color ideas.

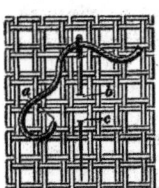
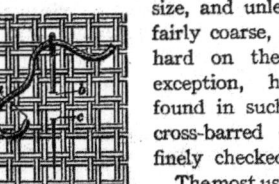
FIG. 1

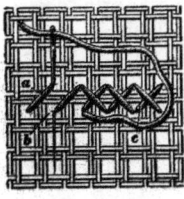
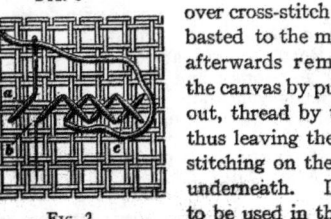
FIG. 2

CROSS-STITCH canvas is a stiff material, resembling scrim and woven with the threads far enough apart to block it off into definite squares. There are two kinds, plain, or single-thread, and Penelope, or double-thread canvas. Both come in a variety of sizes, ranging from 6, 8, or 10 squares to the inch for very coarse work and 12, 16 or even more squares for fine work. All sizes may be used, following the same pattern, each square of the design corresponding to one square of the canvas. To determine how large the finished effect will be, count the squares covered by the entire width and depth of the design and divide each by the number of squares to the inch in the canvas you intend using.

Having determined the size of the design, cut the canvas 1 inch wider each way and locate the square that comes at the exact center. Place this over the center point of the space to be decorated, and when you are very sure the threads of the material and of the canvas run exactly parallel, baste them together around the edges, and, if the space is large, at intervals across the canvas.

You are now ready for the embroidery. Select the thread to fill the squares of the canvas, and choose a long-eyed embroidery needle. It is well to start near the center of the design as there is less danger of making a mistake in counting. It is simpler, too, if one works the large masses of color first and then fills in the smaller spaces.

TO make the cross-stitch, bring the needle up from the wrong side through both the material and the canvas, running it through the center of a large square of the canvas, as at a, Fig. 1, at the left end of a row of stitches to be the same color. Leave an inch of the thread on the wrong side and work over it instead of knotting the thread. Next, bring the needle a block to the right and a block above a, insert it at b, and bring it out at c. Continue in this way until the right end of the row is reached. This leaves diagonal stitches on the right side, as at a, Fig. 2, and vertical ones on the wrong side. Complete the stitches by returning to the starting place, working from right to left and being careful to bring out the needle for each stitch in exactly the point where a stitch of the first row was made, as at b. The completed stitches appear as at c. Take care to have each top stitch cross the lower one in the same direction so that the result is uniform. Only isolated stitches should be completed separately.

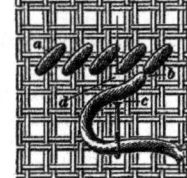
FIG. 3

CROSS-STITCH designs may be used also for needle-point, sometimes termed petit-point, gros-point or tapestry, which is whimsically spoken of as the "half-sister" of cross-stitch, because it is literally half a cross-stitch. Tapestry yarn is usually used for this stitch as it fills in the spaces well, though cottons and silks may also serve.

Fig. 3 shows at a the finished stitch, which is done like the first row of cross-stitch. For the second row, in which the stitches run in the same direction as those of the first, bring the needle out at the lower end of the last stitch of the first row, as at b. Then insert the needle, as at c, one square to the left and below and bring it out in the square above, as at d. The third row is then done like the first.

The pillow illustrated shows a design in wool on black satin, worked over Penelope canvas, having 8 squares to the inch.

Wiping Out the Miles

By ALICE M. STONE
Editorial Department

"THE Woman's Institute came. It wiped out distance. It made each home its influence touched at once a school. And the time for study, each woman's odd moments of convenience."

That claim has been proven two hundred and forty odd thousand times, but perhaps never quite so dramatically as in the experience of Mrs. M. P. Lyman, one of our cookery students.

Two hundred miles out in the Arctic Ocean, fifteen hundred miles by dog team to the nearest accessible railroad, only 1,100 miles from the North Pole, the farthest north a white woman can go, yet the helpful, sympathetic guidance of Institute teachers reached her way out there on the fringe of civilization with as intimate and personal a touch as it reaches the student but a half dozen miles from Scranton.

In effect, her teachers were as close to her as the nearest dog-team station, and this sense of contact with women of her own kind must have reached and warmed a lonely spot in her existence, for on all the island where she stayed, there were but four white women. Even the face of a stranger was an event, for few men reached this strange outpost unless business called them there.

IT was a wonderful experience, though, to make the trip, to see the midnight sun, the midday darkness, the big polar bear, the white foxes, the hair seal swimming around in the water like ducks, the Esquimos, and their poor little hovels, so low that she, though barely 5 feet 3 inches, must stoop to enter them. So she told us in a letter that was carried steadily for seven or eight days by dog teams to Aklavik on the mainland. There it was picked up by other dog teams and kept on going till it reached Ft. McMurray, the end of the steel railroad for Edmonton, *getting in there three months after it was mailed*, a letter that bore not even a postage stamp, for the ship carrying supplies to the Island was lost at sea and postage stamps were not available.

"*We saw the sun today for the first time in seven weeks*," she wrote. "Christmas week we were in total darkness. We can see to get about and it is a little lighter just at noon, but lamps are lit all day."

"It's not as cold as one would think," she added. But scarcely had the ink dried when she announced, "Today it's 40° below zero and one cannot stay out long unless one is used to the cold and dressed for it. Everybody dresses in fur, mostly deer skins. The native women are real experts in sewing fur. It's wonderful to see the way they trim up their coats, sewing for six weeks on one."

Increasing the bleakness of the picture, the ice that's blown off the ocean piles up on the shore ten and fifteen feet high in winter, and in summer huge icebergs come floating in. These are not without their utilitarian value, however, for the ice that's above the water is soft and furnishes ice for use.

Dogs are the only domestic animal. Every native has a team of five, so the Island is alive with them. These beasts of burden are touched with a strain of wolf. Chained when they are not in harness, they make the nights weird with their cries which resemble the wail of the prairie wolf.

BUT with all its strangeness and remoteness, there are poignant reminders of home. In the comfortable, twelve-room house of the Hudson Bay Co., where Mrs. Lyman cooks for ten or twelve employes and fur buyers, there is, for instance, a familiar object that strangely warms and cheers the heart of a home-sick man—a kitchen range.

Despite the great distance of the Island from markets, foodstuffs are plentiful and quite such as one would find in the average American home.

"I have lots of chances to work out my recipes," writes Mrs. Lyman. "We had waffles yesterday and they were lovely. I have the best flour, lard, and baking powder. In fact, all groceries are the best grade. Our vegetables are dried or canned and they are very good indeed. We have 90 dozen eggs packed in salt. They came from Los Angeles this summer, all the way around Alaska, *over four thousand miles*."

AND so it is that one woman has found contentment and usefulness in carrying her knowledge of the home arts into a country that would be singularly desolate without its hearthstones. Surely, her experience is a striking illustration, too, of the extent to which education has been made available to all women. It is just as near as your nearest mail box, or, as in the case of Mrs. Lyman, as her nearest dog-train station.

Which Class Is Yours?
1916 to 1927

"Though we may be widely separated by the miles, we can be united in spirit and heart." These few words from Dorothy Harmeling, the very first Woman's Institute student, voice anew what thousands of others have expressed in letters that have made our students seem very near and very dear to us.

Miss Harmeling's letter to you, enclosed with this issue of INSPIRATION, tells of a plan for an organization of your class. Many of our students have expressed an interest in knowing other members of their class and in developing a school spirit through which these friendships might be strengthened.

How interesting it will be to join with your Institute classmates in this worth-while undertaking! The class spirit that will be created! The officers of your class that will be selected! The permanent Alumnae Association! The special honor that will go to the class that has the largest representation! The year book with the name of each student who participates! And last and best of all, the joy and happiness that this combined effort of all eleven classes will bring to girls and women all over the country.

A friend who frequently visits us, has always seemed to get more enjoyment than most folks out of her college experience. When asked how it was that her college seemed to be so much a part of her life, she said, "Each year since I left I've tried to be represented by some friend that I've influenced to take my place." And so it is all through life. Our greatest happiness comes when we have shared with others what has helped us most.

Read Miss Harmeling's message to you today and then think of the friends you know who need just the help Institute membership brings.

May the Best Class Win and May That Class Be Yours

Our Tenth Anniversary Gifts to YOU

VOLUME 1
225 Pages
74 Illustrations
VOLUME 2
211 Pages
72 Illustrations
VOLUME 3
243 Pages
156 Illustrations
VOLUME 4
245 Pages
127 Illustrations
VOLUME 5
303 Pages
97 Illustrations

Woman's Institute Library of Cookery

Five Handsome, Practical Volumes, 1227 Pages—526 Illustrations, Everything You Want to Know About Foods and Cookery—Regularly sold at $15—Now FREE to You;

or

ANY THREE VOLUMES
of the I.C.S. Technical Library
(See Page Four)

Everything You Have Always Wanted to Know About Planning, Preparing, Serving, Entertaining

Time and again you have heard of the Woman's Institute Library of Cookery. You've wished many times for a set of your own. Now, we bring you the glad news that that wish may be realized—that now you may have this coveted guide to ease and perfection in cookery *without a cent of expense.* For it comes to you, entirely free of cost, as our Anniversary Gift to You, as explained in the inside pages of this folder.

Think of possessing as your very own the textbooks of the complete Woman's Institute Course in Foods and Cookery! Beautifully bound in delft blue, indexed for speedy reference, containing the most thorough instruction on cooking and serving. Answering every conceivable question pertaining to foods and cookery. They should be the indispensable set of books in every student's home, and now through our special Tenth Anniversary Offer it will be possible for every student to own this splendid library.

These books contain more than one thousand proved and tested recipes, presented as recipes never were presented before, through amazingly simple directions and with the aid of hundreds of wonderful step-by-step photographs that entirely eliminate guesswork and show you just exactly what to do. Unlike any other books that have ever been published on this subject, these books cover every phase of the selection, purchase, care, preparation and serving of food of every kind. So, as you learn to prepare each article of food for the table, you learn also its food value, its composition, its place in the diet.

Pictures Make Everything Clear

Drawings and photographs and charts are carried in an interesting and unbroken procession through every section of these splendid books. Graphic pages show how values are distributed in various foods. Cereals, breads of all kinds, milk, butter, eggs and vegetables take their well deserved places in new and delightful recipes. Soups, meats, poultry, game and fish are brought to you in delicious fashions. And the canning, preserving and meal planning sections are constantly proving their worth. Then there are tempting salads, sandwiches, desserts, cakes, puddings, pastries, jellies, confections and beverages to provide in an almost endless series of delightful surprises for all seasons of the year. In fact, no matter what you may wish to know about foods and cookery you will find it, ready and waiting for you, in the Library of Cookery.

These Five Wonderful Volumes FREE

During our Tenth Anniversary Period from January 1st to February 28th, you will have an opportunity to get one of these sets of the Library of Cookery entirely *free.* The offer is fully explained on the next page. We would urge you to take advantage of this opportunity to procure your Library of Cookery, as this will be the last time that such a liberal offer can be made.

Vintage Notions Monthly continues to share the work of Mary Brooks Picken and the Woman's Institute which inspired my book *Vintage Notions*. Although the Institute was founded 100 years ago, the treasure trove of lessons and stories are still relevant today and offer a blueprint for living a contented life.

If you enjoyed this issue of *Vintage Notions Monthly*, visit AmyBarickman.com for more of my curated collection of vintage content including patterns and books for needle and thread, inspiring fabric and textiles & free vintage art every Friday. Be sure to tune in to *Vintage Notions* episodes for a guided tour through my collection of sewing and fashion history, as well as modern projects inspired by my extensive library.

---

www.amybarickman.com
Find free images, inspiration and books for the sewing and needle arts!

www.indygojunction.com
Featuring digital & print patterns, books, tutorials, giveaways, project ideas, & more!

Subscribe to each of our eNewsletters to learn about new products, receive special offers, discounts, videos, and get a FREE eBook!

Vintage Notions Monthly, Volume 1, Issue 9 (VN0109)

All rights reserved. Printed in USA. No part of this publication covered by the copyrights herein may be used in any form or reproduced by any means—graphic, electronic, or mechanical, including photocopying, recording, except for excerpts in the context for reviews, without written permission of the publisher. Purchasing this book represents agreement that the buyer will use this book for personal use only, not for reproduction or resale in whole or in part. The original, rare content is in the public domain;however this restored and revised edition has been created from my personal collection and is protected by copyright.

For wholesale ordering information contact Amy Barickman, LLC at 913.341.5559 or amyb@amybarickman.com, P.O. Box 30238, Kansas City, MO 64112

www.ingramcontent.com/pod-product-compliance
Lightning Source LLC
LaVergne TN
LVHW061256060426
835507LV00020B/2338